Helping a Palestinian State Succeed   KEY FINDINGS

This volume is based on the following studies:

BUILDING A SUCCESSFUL PALESTINIAN STATE

STUDY GROUP DIRECTORS

Steven N. Simon, C. Ross Anthony, Glenn E. Robinson, David C. Gompert, Jerrold D. Green, Robert E. Hunter, C. Richard Neu, Kenneth I. Shine

AUTHORS

Justin L. Adams, Adel K. Afifi, C. Ross Anthony, Cheryl Benard, Mark Bernstein, David Brannan, Rachel Christina, Cynthia R. Cook, Keith Crane, Richard J. Deckelbaum, Kateryna Fonkych, Charles A. Goldman, David G. Groves, Seth G. Jones, Kevin F. McCarthy, Amber Moreen, Brian Nichiporuk, Kevin Jack Riley, Glenn E. Robinson, Michael Schoenbaum, Steven N. Simon, Anga R. Timilsina

THE ARC: A FORMAL STRUCTURE FOR A PALESTINIAN STATE

AUTHORS

Doug Suisman, Steven N. Simon, Glenn E. Robinson, C. Ross Anthony, Michael Schoenbaum

Supported by a gift from David and Carol Richards; by a gift from Guilford Glazer; and by RAND discretionary funds, which are provided by donors and earnings on research contracts

RAND
CORPORATION

Primary funding for the research described in this report was provided by private individuals. Funding for *Building a Successful Palestinian State* was provided by a generous gift from David and Carol Richards. *The Arc: A Formal Structure for a Palestinian State* was initiated by Guilford Glazer and funded by his generous gift. This research in the public interest was also supported by RAND, using discretionary funds made possible by the generosity of RAND's other donors and the earnings on client-funded research.

Library of Congress Cataloging-in-Publication Data

Helping a Palestinian state succeed : key findings.
    p. cm.
    "MG-146/1."
    ISBN 0-8330-3771-4 (pbk. : alk. paper)
    1. Arab-Israeli conflict—1993– —Peace. 2. Palestine—Politics and government. 3. National security—Palestine. 4. Palestine—Economic conditions. 5. Palestine—Population. I. Rand Corporation.

DS119.76.H457 2005
956.05'3—dc22
                                              2005005258

The RAND Corporation is a nonprofit research organization providing objective analysis and effective solutions that address the challenges facing the public and private sectors around the world. RAND's publications do not necessarily reflect the opinions of its research clients and sponsors.

RAND® is a registered trademark.

Cover design by Ph.D, www.phdla.com
Background image: Asalah Magazine. Porthole photos: (first three): Photos courtesy
Pere Vidal i Domènech; (far right): "The Olive Tree: Hi Mama, I'm Home!" Photo courtesy
Steve Sabella at www.sabellaphoto.com
Figures on pp. 16, 18, 21–23, and 25–26 courtesy Suisman Urban Design

Published 2005 by the RAND Corporation
1776 Main Street, P.O. Box 2138, Santa Monica, CA 90407-2138
1200 South Hayes Street, Arlington, VA 22202-5050
201 North Craig Street, Suite 202, Pittsburgh, PA 15213-1516
RAND URL: http://www.rand.org/
To order RAND documents or to obtain additional information, contact
Distribution Services: Telephone: (310) 451-7002;
Fax: (310) 451-6915; Email: order@rand.org

Preface

The Palestinian Authority, Israel, the United States, the European Union, Russia, and the United Nations all officially support the establishment of an independent Palestinian state. Since the death of Yasser Arafat and the recent elections in Gaza and the West Bank, there has been interest in many quarters in renewing the peace process.

This document summarizes research conducted by the RAND Corporation to develop recommendations, based on rigorous analysis, about steps that Palestinians, Israel, the United States, and the international community could take if a Palestinian state were established to promote the state's success. This work is described in detail in two separate publications: *Building a Successful Palestinian State* and *The Arc: A Formal Structure for a Palestinian State*. A forthcoming companion report, entitled *Building a Successful Palestinian State: Security,* examines security issues in more detail.

In the first two studies, RAND developed initial cost estimates for implementing its recommendations. The estimates, summarized at the end of this document, suggest that the funding necessary to implement RAND's recommendations is within the capacity of combined international resources and private investors. Although RAND's analyses assume a peace accord, many of the recommendations in both studies could be implemented immediately.

This work should be of interest to the Palestinian and Israeli communities; to Palestinian government officials; to policymakers in the Roadmap Quartet (the United States, the European Union, the United Nations, and Russia); to foreign policy experts; and to organizations and individuals committed to helping establish and sustain a successful state of Palestine. It should also be of interest to the negotiating teams charged with the responsibility of establishing the new state.

Principal research for these studies was carried out from September 2002 through September 2004 by multidisciplinary teams of RAND researchers, working under the direction of the RAND Health Center for Domestic and International Health Security and the Center for Middle East Public Policy (CMEPP), one of

RAND's international programs. RAND Health and CMEPP are units of the RAND Corporation.

Primary funding for the projects was provided by private individuals. Funding for *Building a Successful Palestinian State* was provided by a generous gift from David and Carol Richards. *The Arc: A Formal Structure for a Palestinian State* was initiated by Guilford Glazer and funded by his generous gift. This research in the public interest was also supported by RAND, using discretionary funds made possible by the generosity of RAND's other donors and the earnings on client-funded research.

Contents

Figures

CHAPTER ONE

Introduction

From September 2002 through September 2004, RAND conducted two studies that focused on the question of how an independent Palestinian state could be made successful.

The first study surveyed a wide range of political, economic, social, and environmental challenges that a new Palestinian state would face, in order to identify policy options that Palestinians, Israelis, and the international community could adopt to promote the state's success. Building on RAND's first study, our second study explored options for addressing the housing, transportation, and related infrastructure needs of a burgeoning Palestinian population. The second study explicitly considers issues related to potential immigration to a new Palestinian state of a substantial number of diaspora Palestinian refugees.

This Executive Summary presents the highlights of both studies. Readers in search of more information should consult the respective volumes:

RAND Corporation, Palestinian State Study Group (Steven N. Simon, C. Ross Anthony, Glenn E. Robinson et al.), *Building a Successful Palestinian State,* Santa Monica, Calif.: The RAND Corporation, MG-146-DCR, 2005.

Doug Suisman, Steven N. Simon, Glenn E. Robinson, C. Ross Anthony, and Michael Schoenbaum, *The Arc: A Formal Structure for a Palestinian State,* Santa Monica, Calif.: RAND Corporation, MG-327-GG, 2005.

CHAPTER TWO

Building a Successful Palestinian State

Identifying the requirements for success is a pressing policy need if a new Palestinian state is established. A critical mass of Palestinians and Israelis, as well as the United States, Russia, the European Union, and the United Nations, remains committed to the establishment of a Palestinian state. The "Roadmap" initiative, which all these parties officially endorsed, originally called for the establishment of a new Palestinian state by 2005.[1] President Bush recently revised this timetable for the United States, calling for a new state by 2009. Although prospects for an independent Palestine are uncertain, recent history in nation-building clearly indicates that in the absence of detailed plans, such efforts almost always fail.

RAND explored options for structuring the institutions of a future Palestinian state, so as to promote the state's chances of success. We did not examine how the parties could reach a settlement that would create an independent Palestinian state. Rather, we developed recommendations, based on objective analysis, about steps that Palestinians, Israel, the United States, and the international community can take now, and when an independent Palestinian state is created, to increase the likelihood that the new state will succeed.

Nation-building is a very difficult undertaking, even under less challenging conditions. Even if a peace is agreed to, significant distrust will remain between Palestinians and Israelis, and dissidents in both countries—and from the outside—are likely to try to disrupt progress toward a successful Palestinian state. Success will require good planning; significant resources; fortitude; major and sustained involvement of the international community; and courage, commitment, and hard work on the part of the Palestinian people.

---

[1] The full title of the Roadmap is *A Performance-Based Roadmap to a Permanent Two-State Solution to the Israeli-Palestinian Conflict* and can be found at http://www.state.gov/r/pa/ei/rls/22520.htm, as of February 2005.

Approach

In our analysis, we first considered the essentials of a successful new state, particularly the nature of the institutions that will govern it and the structures and processes that will maintain security. We then described the demographic, economic, and environmental resources on which a Palestinian state can draw and also identified factors that can limit the state's ability to use these resources effectively. Finally, we considered what a Palestinian state must do to ensure that its citizens are healthy and educated.

In each substantive area, we drew on the best available empirical data to describe the requirements for success, to identify alternative policies for achieving these requirements, and to analyze the consequences of choosing different alternatives. For most of the areas, we also estimated the financial costs associated with implementing our recommendations over the first decade of independence. Costs are presented in constant 2003 U.S. dollars, with no attempt to adjust the estimates for future trends in inflation or exchange rates. The costing methodology differed with the nature of the analytic questions and the availability of data.

These estimates are not based on detailed cost analyses. Rather, we intend them to suggest the scale of financial assistance that will be required from the international community to help develop a successful Palestinian state. More-precise estimates will require formal cost studies involving detailed needs assessments. Nor did we estimate the costs of all the major institutional changes and improvements in infrastructure that would be required for a successful Palestinian state.

Defining Success

In our view, "success" in Palestine will require an independent, democratic state with an effective government operating under the rule of law in a safe and secure environment that provides for economic development and supports adequate housing, food, education, health, and public services for its people. To achieve this success, Palestine must address four fundamental challenges:

- **Security:** Palestinian statehood must improve the level of security for Palestinians, Israelis, and the region.
- **Governance:** A Palestinian state must govern effectively and be viewed as legitimate by both its citizens and the international community.
- **Economic development:** Palestine must be economically viable and, over time, self-reliant.
- **Well-being of its people:** Palestine must be capable of feeding, clothing, educating, and providing for the health and social well-being of its people.

Conditions for Success

Security

The success of an independent Palestinian state is inconceivable in the absence of peace and security for Palestinians and Israelis alike. Adequate security is a prerequisite to achieving all other recommendations stemming from our analysis. An independent Palestinian state must be secure within its borders, provide for the routine safety of its inhabitants, be free from subversion or foreign exploitation, and pose no threat to Israel. Moreover, these conditions must be established from the moment of independence: Unlike infrastructure or industry, security is not something that can be built gradually.

Successful security arrangements range from protecting borders that surround the state to maintaining law and order within it. Success, even under the most favorable conditions, will probably require extensive international assistance and close cooperation among security personnel.

Governance

Good governance will be a key measure of the new state's success. From our perspective, that must include governance that represents the will of the people, practices the rule of law, and is virtually free of corruption. The government must also enjoy the support of the people. To gain that support, the new state must be seen as legitimate in the eyes of Palestinians and practice the good governance that is necessary to maintain public respect and support. The thoroughness with which democratic institutions and processes, including the rule of law, are established will be vital from the outset—indeed, they are already critical even before the state has been created.

Economic Development

An independent Palestinian state cannot be considered successful unless its people have good economic opportunities and quality of life. Palestinian economic development has historically been constrained, and per-capita national income peaked in the late 1990s in the range of "lower middle income" countries (as defined by the World Bank). Since then, national income has fallen by half or more following the start of the second intifada ("uprising") against Israel in September 2000. An independent Palestinian state will need to improve economic conditions for its people just as urgently as it will need to improve security conditions.

Our analysis indicated that Palestine can succeed only with the backing, resources, and support of the international community—above all, the United States, the European Union, the United Nations, the World Bank, and the International Monetary Fund. Resource requirements will be substantial for a decade or more. However, the availability of such resources cannot be assumed. This limited availability of resources intensifies the need for the state to succeed quickly, especially in the eyes of those who might provide private investment capital.

During the period of international assistance, the Palestinian state should invest aid, not merely consume it. Ultimately, an independent Palestinian state cannot be characterized as successful until the state becomes largely self-reliant.

Social Well-Being

A fourth condition for the success of an independent Palestinian state is that the living conditions of its people improve substantially over time. Many observers have suggested that disappointment about slow improvement in living conditions under Palestinian administration after 1994—and sharp declines in some years—may have contributed significantly to the outbreak of the second intifada.

In addition to the conditions for success described above, the Palestinian health and education systems must be strengthened. Both systems start with considerable strengths. But both will also need considerable development, which will require effective governance and economic growth, as well as external technical and financial assistance.

In the area of health, the state can be seen as successful if it is able to provide its citizens with access to adequate primary, secondary, and tertiary care services while being able to carry out the essential public health functions of a modern state, including immunization programs for children. In education, all children need to be assured access to educational opportunities to enable them to achieve their potential while contributing to the economic and social well-being of the society.

Crosscutting Issues: Contiguity, Permeability, and Security

Our analysis identified three crosscutting issues that will strongly influence prospects for the success of a Palestinian state:

- whether the state's territory (apart from the separation of Gaza from the West Bank) is *contiguous*
- how freely people can move between Israel and an independent Palestinian state, which we refer to as "*permeability*" of borders
- the prevailing degree of *security* and public safety.

These issues affect all of the other issues examined in RAND's analyses. It is important to understand how they are interlinked, how they affect key goals, and how they might be reconciled.

Contiguity of Territory

Palestinian political legitimacy and economic viability will depend in large measure on contiguity of land. A Palestine of enclaves is likely to fail. Political and social development requires that Palestinians be free to move within and among Palestinian territories. Successful economic development requires that movement of goods within and among Palestinian territories be as free as possible.

Permeability of Borders

Permeability of borders is basic to the new state's near-term economic viability. Movement of people between Israel and Palestine will be crucial to the Palestinian economy by giving labor, products, and services access to a vibrant market and by encouraging foreign investment in Palestine. However, permeability must be balanced with security concerns for Israel.

Security

Security is a precondition for successful establishment and development of all other aspects of a Palestinian state. One critical dimension of security is the confidence of Palestinian citizens that they live under the rule of law. A second key dimension is protection against political violence.

We concluded that none of the major conditions of success—security, good governance, economic viability, social welfare—can be realized unless Palestinian territory is substantially contiguous. In a territorially noncontiguous state, poverty would aggravate political discontent and create a situation where maintaining security would be all but impossible. In addition, a Palestine divided into several or many parts would present a complex security challenge since a noncontiguous state would hamper law enforcement coordination; require duplicative and, therefore, expensive capabilities; and risk spawning rivalries among security officials, as happened between Gaza and the West Bank under the Palestinian Authority. Greater border permeability is essential for economic development but significantly complicates security.

Key Findings from the Analyses

Governance

A successful Palestinian state will be characterized by good governance, including a commitment to democracy and the rule of law. A precondition to good governance is that the state's citizens view their leaders as legitimate. Ultimately, the new state's political support and legitimacy will depend on an array of conditions, including the form and effectiveness of governance, economic and social development, territorial size and its contiguity, the status of Jerusalem, and the freedom of refugees to resettle in Palestine.

Good governance will be more easily achieved if Palestine's borders are open, its economy prosperous, its refugee absorption manageable, its security guaranteed, and its early years bolstered by significant international assistance. Good governance will not be achieved without significant effort and international assistance and will most likely come by reforming the present government institutions and practices. At a minimum, Palestine must adopt actions that (1) promote the rule of law including empowering the judiciary, (2) shift some power from the executive to the legislative branches of Palestinian government, (3) significantly reduce corruption, (4) promote meritocracy in the civil service, and (5) delegate power to local officials. A pending constitution that recognizes the will of the people and clearly defines the powers of various branches of government must be wisely completed. Finally, the authoritarian practices and corruption that in the past have characterized rule under the Palestinian Authority must be eliminated.

Strengthening Palestinian governance will entail real financial costs, for instance for conducting elections, and for establishing and operating the legislative and executive branches of government. We did not explicitly estimate the costs of these institutional changes. However, in some instances, they are addressed in the analysis of the other sectors.

Internal Security

The most pressing internal security concern for a Palestinian state will be the need to suppress militant organizations that pose a grave threat to both interstate security (through attacks against Israel and international forces) and intrastate security (through violent opposition to legitimate authority). Public safety and routine law enforcement—administration of justice—will also need to be put on a sound footing as quickly as possible.

Assistance for the administration of justice would facilitate the emergence of an independent judiciary and an efficient law enforcement agency capable of investigating and countering common criminal activity and ensuring public safety. Both of these broad objectives would require funds for rebuilding courthouses and police stations, legal texts, computers, forensic and other training, and the kind of equipment that police need to carry out their day-to-day patrolling duties. A more comprehensive program aimed at accelerating the reform process and creating a sense of security for Palestinian citizens more swiftly would include deploying international police and vetting and recruiting judges, prosecutors, and police officers.

As in the realms of counterterrorism and counterintelligence, internal security requirements would demand restructuring the security services and up-to-date equipment, monitoring, training, and analytical support. Depending on the severity of the domestic terrorist threat and the speed with which Palestinian capacities develop in this area, a more intensive program might be needed.

We estimate general reconstruction costs related to internal security to be at least $600 million per year, and as much as $7.7 billion over ten years.

Demography

There are almost 9 million Palestinians, nearly 40 percent of them living within the boundaries of what is likely to become a new Palestinian state (the West Bank and Gaza). The population's fertility rate is very high. If there is large-scale immigration by diaspora Palestinians, the population in the Palestinian territories will grow very rapidly for the foreseeable future.

Rapid population growth will stretch the state's ability to provide water, sewerage, and transportation to Palestinian residents and increase the costs of doing so. It will tax the physical and human capital required to provide education, health, and housing and place a heavy financial burden for funding these services on a disproportionately smaller working-age population. A new Palestinian state will also be hard-pressed to provide jobs for the rapidly growing number of young adults who will be entering the labor force.

There are clear signs that Palestinian fertility rates are declining, but the rate of decline is uncertain. In the short run, births will certainly increase since the number of Palestinian women in the prime childbearing years will more than double. Over the longer term, fertility rates will begin to decline. How much these declines will lower the total fertility rate probably depends on the degree to which the education levels and labor force participation of Palestinian women rise.

There is also considerable uncertainty surrounding the number of diaspora Palestinians who might move to a new Palestinian state. The Palestinian Central Bureau of Statistics and the United States Census Bureau estimate between 100,000 and 500,000 returnees. Our own estimates, based on assumptions about which groups of Palestinians will be most likely to return and under what conditions, are somewhat higher. Ultimately, the number of Palestinians returning will depend upon the terms of the final agreement and on social, political, and economic developments in the new Palestinian state. These demographic realities greatly affect the likely economic and social development of any new state.

Water

A viable Palestinian state will need adequate supplies of clean water for domestic consumption, commercial and industrial development, and agriculture. These requirements are not being met today. Current water and waste management practices are degrading both surface streams and rivers and underground water resources.

Most of Palestine's water is provided by springs and wells fed by underground aquifers that are shared with Israel. Current water resource development provides only about one-half of the World Health Organization's per-capita domestic water requirement and limits irrigation and food production. In addition, current water use is unsustainable: The amount of water that the Palestinians and Israelis extract from most of the region's aquifers exceeds the natural replenishment rate.

Options we examined for increasing the water supply included increasing groundwater use, accommodated by Israel's reduction in use; increasing rain and storm water capture; and increasing desalination capabilities where no other options exist. Demand can be managed through smart application of water efficiency technologies, water reuse methods, and infrastructure improvements.

We estimate a cost of more than $4.9 billion for supplying water and sanitation for the decade through 2014. Improved water management strategies could reduce this amount by up to $1.3 billion to $2 billion.

Health

The health system of a future Palestinian state starts with many strengths, including a relatively healthy population, a high societal value placed on health, many highly qualified health professionals, national plans for health system development, and a strong base of governmental and nongovernmental institutions.

Important areas of concern include poor system-wide coordination and implementation of policies and programs across geographic areas and between the governmental and nongovernmental sectors of the health system, many underqualified health care providers, weak systems for licensing and continuing education, and considerable deficits in the operating budgets of the Palestinian Ministry of Health and the government health insurance system (the principal source of health insurance).

Our analysis focused on major institutions that the health care system would need in the first decade of an independent state. In addition, we identified several urgently needed programs for preventive and curative care.

We recommend that priority be given to initiatives in two areas:

- Integrating health system planning and policy development more closely, with meaningful input from all relevant governmental and nongovernmental stakeholders.
- Improving public and primary health care programs, including an updated immunization program, comprehensive micronutrient fortification and supplementation, prevention and treatment of chronic and noninfectious disease, and treatment of developmental and psychosocial conditions.

We estimate that the Palestinian health system could constructively absorb between $125 million and $160 million per year in external (international) support over the first decade of an independent state.

Education

The future state's education system begins with a strong foundation, especially in the areas of access, quality, and delivery. Access strengths include a commitment to equitable access and success in achieving gender parity, strong community support for education, and leadership that is supportive of both system expansion and system reform. Strengths in the area of quality include willingness to engage in curricular reform; strong interest in and resources for improving pedagogy; commitment to improving the qualifications and compensation of staff; and the perception of schools as a key location for developing students' civic skills and social responsibility. The system is relatively well managed and has solid data collection capabilities.

Nevertheless, the system faces notable challenges. In the area of access, these include rising levels of malnutrition, homelessness, and general poor health; inadequate facilities and supplies; unsafe schools and routes to schools; lack of special education options for students with special needs; lack of nonformal education options for school-age students; and the absence of lifelong learning opportunities. Quality challenges include a lack of clear goals and expectations for the system; limited relevance of secondary, vocational, and tertiary programs; limited research and development capacity and activity; low staff compensation and an emerging administrative "bulge"; and difficulty in monitoring process and outcomes. Delivery is hobbled by a severely underfunded and donor-dependent system, and the limited data on the system are not effectively linked to reform.

Our analysis examined ways in which access, quality, and delivery could be improved, with a long-term goal of positioning Palestine as a powerful player in the region's knowledge economy. We recommend an array of activities within three primary goals for the system over the next ten years:

- Maintaining currently high levels of access, while also working within resource constraints to expand enrollments in secondary education (particularly in vocational and technical education and the academic science track) and early childhood programs.
- Building quality by focusing on integrated curricular standards, assessments, and professional development, supported by long-term planning for system sustainability.
- Improving delivery by working with donors to develop streamlined and integrated funding mechanisms that allow school administrations to focus on the business of meeting student needs.

We estimate that the Palestinian education system will require between $1 billion and $1.5 billion per year in financing over the first decade of statehood if it is to operate at a level that will support national ambitions for development. (We do not distinguish between donor and national investments.) We recognize that these investment levels are substantial, both in absolute terms and relative to historical spending levels in Palestine (which averaged around $250 million per year during 1996–1999). Our recommendations are based on international benchmarks for spending per pupil in successful education systems. We also offer options for reducing costs should it be necessary to do so.

Economic Development

We examined possible economic development trajectories in an independent Palestinian state during the 2005 to 2019 time frame, focusing on Palestine's prospects for sustaining growth in per-capita incomes. Prerequisites for successful economic development include adequate security, good governance, adequate and contiguous territory, stable access to adequate supplies of power and water, and an adequate transportation infrastructure. In addition to the prerequisites, four critical issues— transaction costs; resources, including internal resources and financing and external aid; the Palestinian trade regime; and the access of Palestinian labor to employment in Israel—will primarily determine the conditions under which the Palestinian economy will function.

Since Palestinian territory has limited natural resources, economic development will depend critically on human capital, with stronger systems of primary, secondary, and vocational education as indispensable down payments on any future economic success. Other important conditions will include Palestinian access to Israeli labor markets and substantial freedom of movement of people and products across the state's borders, including the border with Israel. However, brittle Israeli-Palestinian relations are likely to constrain cross-border movement of Palestinians into Israel for some time after a peace agreement.

Strategic choices made by policymakers at the outset of the new state will markedly affect its economic development. Decisions about *geographic contiguity*—the size, shape, and fragmentation of a future Palestinian state, the inclusion of special sites or areas, and control over land and resources—will determine the resources that the new state's leaders will have to foster growth and the ease with which Palestinians can move and engage in business. Decisions about the degree of *economic integration* with Israel in terms of trade and the mobility of Palestinian labor will shape the Palestinian economy, the rate of economic growth, and prospects for employment.

We believe that a future Palestinian state could develop within the confines of four scenarios, determined by decisions about geographic contiguity (high versus low) and economic integration with Israel (high versus low). We estimated the levels of economic growth that might be achieved under each scenario, given specific levels of international investment. Not surprisingly, our analyses confirm the value for economic development of a high degree of geographic contiguity and of a high degree of economic integration with Israel. A highly contiguous Palestine—one with fewer impediments to the movement of goods and people—would have lower transaction costs and a broader base of economic activity. A Palestine that has open borders and liberal trade policies with Israel would enable Palestinians to access lucrative employment opportunities in Israel as well as provide customers for Palestinian raw materials and intermediate goods exports.

Under each scenario except the low-contiguity/low-integration case, Palestine could reasonably surpass its 1999 per-capita gross national income by 2009 and double it by 2019. However, such economic growth presupposes very significant investment in Palestinian capital stock: Between 2005 and 2019, the Palestinian private and public sectors and the international community would have to invest about $3.3 billion annually, for a cumulative total of some $33 billion over the first decade of independence (and $50 billion over the period 2005–2019).

Under any scenario, domestic private employment would have to grow at a substantial pace (perhaps at an annual average of 15 to 18 percent) between 2005 and 2009 to reach rates of employment last seen near the summer of 2000. These employment rates should be possible once Palestinian businesses are able to operate in a relatively unrestricted environment and are fully able to utilize available resources.

Our analysis also identified a number of best-practice policies to encourage economic development and growth in per-capita incomes. These policies should involve efforts to repair and invest in Palestinian infrastructure pertaining to transportation, water, power, and communications; this infrastructure forms the basis of any functioning economy. They should also involve efforts to nurture economic activity. Critical areas include fostering free trade between Palestine and elsewhere by minimizing the costs of commerce; joining with Palestine's neighbors to develop specific economic sectors; expanding access to capital through a program of industrial and economic development zones, reformed domestic banking policies, and an international insurance fund; and improving the business climate through increased transparency and accountability of Palestinian governance.

Implementing These Recommendations

Many of the recommendations we have described could be implemented immediately. All of these issues will be important to consider when a new Palestinian state is agreed upon.

CHAPTER THREE

The Arc: A Formal Structure for a Palestinian State

RAND's first study, *Building a Successful Palestinian State*, analyzed a wide range of political, economic, social, and environmental challenges that a new Palestinian state would face, and described policy options in these areas for facilitating the state's success. RAND's second study, *The Arc: A Formal Structure for a Palestinian State*, builds on the initial study by providing a detailed vision for strengthening the physical infrastructure of a Palestinian state. This vision is designed to address one of the key challenges described in RAND's first study: that of providing for the physical and economic well-being of Palestine's rapidly growing population by providing adequate housing, transportation, and economic opportunity.

The population of the West Bank and Gaza, currently around 3.6 million people, is growing very rapidly due to a high birthrate. Moreover, following independence, the population of Palestine is generally expected to expand further because of immigration. As a working estimate for the present analysis, we assume that the population will grow to approximately 6.6 million by 2020: approximately 2.4 million new people from natural population growth, plus net migration of approximately 600,000 people. We expect immigration to come principally from Palestinian refugees currently living in Lebanon, Syria, and Jordan. Thus Palestine's infrastructure, inadequate even for current needs, will soon be called upon to support perhaps twice as many people. (Palestinian demographic trends, including the issue of returning refugees, are discussed in detail in *Building a Successful Palestinian State*.)

Every nation-state has a shape, which is most immediately recognized by the contours of its international borders. But within those borders there is another shape we might call the nation's formal structure—the pattern of constructed human habitation and human movement, set in relationship to the natural environment. The potential formal structure of a new Palestinian state is the focus of RAND's second project.

In addition to describing options for developing the physical infrastructure of a Palestinian state to meet the needs of its growing population, we also consider some of the key social and political challenges that will be presented by the return to the new state of large numbers of Palestinian refugees and other immigrants currently living abroad.

The Shape of Palestine

We began by examining current patterns of habitation in Palestine. Palestinian villages, towns, and cities are not evenly distributed across the West Bank but are grouped almost entirely in its western half. This clearly reflects topography and climate (see Figure 1). The region is cut in half from north to south by a slightly curving line, or "arc," of mountain ridges. In some areas, the ridgeline reaches more than 3,000 feet above sea level, with more typical heights ranging between 2,000 and 2,500 feet. Because of the prevailing winds from west to east off of the Mediterranean Sea, the West Bank experiences the storm pattern typical of "West Coast Mediterranean" climate zones (from California to South Africa), whereby the rising elevation of the mountains causes most rain to drop on the westerly face of the ridgeline, leaving the eastern face relatively dry. The ridgeline also puts the eastern slopes in a "wind shadow," making them not only dryer but also hotter. This helps explain why Palestinian habitation has remained generally in the west of the West Bank, with its significantly higher rainfall, arable land, and occasional cooling breezes. The notable exception to this pattern is the low-lying oasis of Jericho, whose plentiful and accessible underground water supply has sustained an ancient town in an otherwise inhospitably hot and arid territory.

Figure 1
A Natural Arc

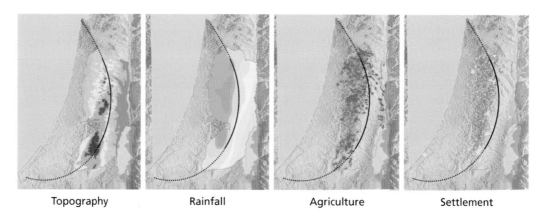

| Topography | Rainfall | Agriculture | Settlement |

The West Bank is divided down its middle by a slightly curving north-south line, or "arc," of mountain ridges. The ridges divide the Mediterranean ecosystem to the west from the arid slopes on the east. Because rainfall is significantly higher on the western side, agriculture is concentrated there, along with the great majority of historic Palestinian settlements.

The *Atlas of Palestine*[2] identifies a family of 11 principal cities in the West Bank. They are, from north to south: Jenin, Tubas, Tulkarm, Nablus, Qalqilya, Salfit, Ramallah, Jericho, Jerusalem, Bethlehem, and Hebron. With the exceptions of Tulkarm and Qalqilya in the west and Jericho in the east, they are loosely arrayed along or near the path of the ridgeline arc. The three largest in population are Jerusalem (250,000), Hebron (154,000), and Nablus (127,000). The next two largest—Tulkarm and Qalqilya—are considerably smaller, with just over 40,000 each.

Many of these cities have been settled for millennia—notably Hebron, Bethlehem, Jerusalem, Jericho, and Nablus—and there are ancient roadways that connect them; indeed, the current path of Route 60, the north-south highway of the West Bank, follows quite closely the ancient route that linked these cities. However, Route 60 today is for the most part relatively narrow, winding, and slow, reflecting a historical preference for north-south travel along the flatter route along the Mediterranean coast and a general lack of investment in upgrading the West Bank's infrastructure. Future economic development in Palestine clearly requires the creation of rapid north-south transportation links for goods and people in the West Bank, and between the West Bank and Gaza.

The discussion of existing conditions cannot conclude without addressing the numerous Israeli settlements in the West Bank and the roads built to serve them. These constitute an essentially autonomous urban system, and their location and design depart from historical building patterns in the region. For these reasons, and because their ultimate political disposition is uncertain, we have chosen for the purposes of this study to set the question of Israeli settlements aside.

Population Density and Options for Growth

With more than 3.6 million people in just over 2,300 square miles, Palestine today has more than 1,400 people per square mile. This population density puts it near the top of the world's densest nations. Europe's densest country, the Netherlands, has 1,200 people per square mile, while Israel has 770 people per square mile and Lebanon 870. The world's densest large country, Bangladesh, has 2,200. If Palestine's population increases, as expected, to more than 6 million within the next 15 years, its density will reach 2,400 people per square mile, exceeding even that of Bangladesh.

High population density is often associated with overcrowding, poverty, disease, traffic congestion, economic anemia, and environmental degradation. However, high population density by itself is not necessarily a prescription for national failure. Indeed, there is something of a reverse correlation when measuring the density of cities as opposed to the density of nations. A growing body of thought and research sug-

---

[2] *Atlas of Palestine,* Jerusalem (Bethlehem): Applied Research Institute, 2002.

gests that in a number of domains—sustainability, environmental performance, reduced energy consumption, livability, even social equity—cities with higher densities may perform better than those with lower densities.

While many cities in Australia and the United States—such as Houston, Phoenix, Adelaide, and Brisbane—have typical average metropolitan densities of around 3,000 people per square mile, thriving Asian and European cities such as Singapore, Paris, and Munich have densities at least ten times as high, averaging 30,000 people per square mile across their metropolitan areas. The successful high-density development of such cities is associated with compact urban form, high-density housing, and good public transportation. The current and projected high population density of a Palestinian state, if combined with certain patterns of higher-density urban development and public transportation, could be an asset in the search for a sustainable formal structure for the state.

Given the location, size, and linkages of existing Palestinian towns and cities, we can consider different options for expanding areas of Palestinian habitation to accommodate millions of additional people. There are many different models of urban distribution within a region; the study team chose to focus on four distinct models for consideration (see Figure 2).

Figure 2
Four Possible Population Distribution Models

| "Hub" model | "Tripod" model | "Net" model | "Linear" model |
| (single mega-city) | (three large cities) | (scattered towns and cities) | (chain of many cities) |

The advantages and disadvantages of four different population distribution models were assessed. The first two were eliminated because of the lack of needed land and risk of overcrowding. The third model distributed benefits widely but had the highest cost with respect to linking infrastructure. The fourth had the widest distribution of benefit and greatest regional integration at the least cost for linking infrastructure, while corresponding most closely to the natural arc in the landscape.

The first is the "hub" model of a single mega-city. The creation of a new city has the potential advantages of centralized development and control on an open landscape, with many opportunities to create strong and positive symbols for the state. But it also entails tremendous logistical, political, and economic challenges. Moreover, the team believes that sufficient contiguous, buildable, and suitable land for such a city is most likely not available in the West Bank.

The second is the "tripod" model of three large cities, specifically Jerusalem, Hebron, and Nablus. Such an approach could mitigate some of the logistical, political, and economic disadvantages of the "hub" model. However, the team remains concerned that even dividing a new population of three million people to three areas may result in cities that are overly crowded and unable to support the demand, and that insufficient buildable land would be available to pursue this course successfully.

The third is a "net" model of scattered towns and cities. Distributing new growth more or less evenly all across the West Bank is attractive in concept, because it spreads the burdens and benefits of growth equally. But scattered development probably requires the most miles of infrastructure at the highest cost. Indeed so much connective infrastructure would be required that setting national priorities would be very challenging and expensive. Also, such distributed growth may encourage political "balkanization," undermining larger regional and national institutions and initiatives.

The fourth is a "linear" model of a chain of multiple cities. The geography and population distribution of the West Bank suggest connecting most of the major cities along a single trunk line, which could cover much of the population relatively efficiently. The chain of cities could provide focus and direction for new economic development while helping to revitalize the principal existing historic centers. By encouraging each urban area to grow in a linear—or "branch"—form to link to the national trunk line, compact and sustainable urban form is favored over undirected and unbounded growth. The approach relates growth to existing topographic and habitation patterns, with the potential to create a strong national symbol through the connective infrastructure itself, rather than exclusively through expensive and possibly wasteful individual architectural monuments. The disadvantages of this approach are that it may favor central areas of the West Bank at the expense of the eastern and western zones and that, if incorrectly implemented, it may create too much urban development along the line of the arc itself. On the basis of this analysis, the team selected the "linear" model as having the most promise for further investigation.

Growth in Gaza

In developing plans to accommodate substantial population growth in Palestine, one obvious step is to propose minimizing the burden of growth in Gaza. Although Gaza will clearly experience substantial natural population growth over the next decades, the population density there is already 9,200 people per square mile. Because of this high initial population density, the relative scarcity of open land, and Gaza's physical separation from the West Bank, we decided that urban planning in Gaza required a substantively different approach than the vision we developed for the West Bank. Efforts in Gaza should therefore focus on the construction of the new international airport and seaport, the linkage of the ports to the West Bank via the transport facilities of the Arc, the development of new infrastructure for seaside tourism, and the physical and economic rehabilitation of the urbanized areas of Gaza. Population and urban growth, on the other hand, should be directed to the West Bank.

Linking the Cities

The "linear" model puts an emphasis on the existing chain of cities along the central spine of the West Bank. Population growth and urban development would be directed to this line. The immediate question raised is how the cities would be linked to each other.

The historic centers of most of the cities are already linked by the roadway called Route 60. This route, however, is inadequate for the future needs of the state. Traffic on the road is necessarily slowed as each metropolitan area is approached and entered. For those traveling longer distances, the route itself may disappear on the south side of the city, only to reappear on the north.

The need for a north-south link and the presence of the north-south arc in the topographic landscape create the intriguing prospect of a major new project parallel to the path of the arc. The primary function of such a project would be to provide the major transportation link for the West Bank (see Figure 3) via frequent, reliable, and high-speed rail service between the primary cities of the West Bank and ultimately to the international airport and cities in Gaza. The total length of this link from Jenin south to Hebron would be approximately 70 miles, while the extension to Gaza would be an additional 60 miles.

The construction of the transportation line would invite the concurrent parallel construction of other needed lines for electricity, natural gas, telecommunications, and water (see Figure 4). A national linear park could weave back and forth across the line as influenced by the landscape. The ensemble could have great symbolic power for the new nation. We call the entirety simply the "Arc."

While a rail line would be the centerpiece of the national infrastructure, rail cannot provide all the needed types of transport. On the passenger side, there will always be a demand for swift automobile linkages via highway—not only for those residents who can afford a car but also for tourists, dignitaries, government officials,

Figure 3
Interurban Rail Line

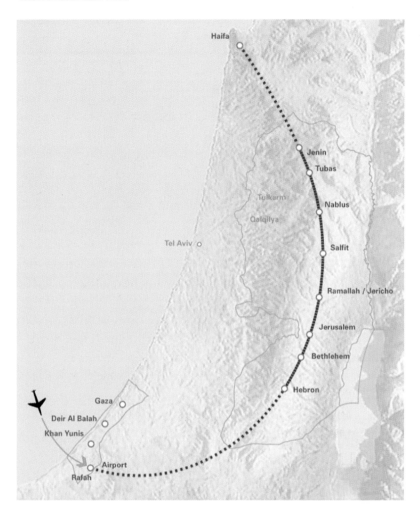

The critical infrastructure along the Arc is a fast interurban rail line linking almost all the primary cities of Gaza and the West Bank—including a stop at the
international airport—in just over 90 minutes. The rail line makes public transportation a national priority while establishing the "trunk" of the national infrastructure corridor.

etc. The demand will also exist for the providers of emergency services, security and
military units, and service and repair vehicles of all kinds. Also, although the Arc
should include capacity to move freight by rail, a significant percentage of freight is
likely to be carried by truck, from small shipments in vans to shipping containers di-
rectly offloaded onto tractor-trailers. This freight traffic will require good roads as
well. To address these needs in a way that is consistent with the Arc's broader devel-

Figure 4
Five Infrastructures

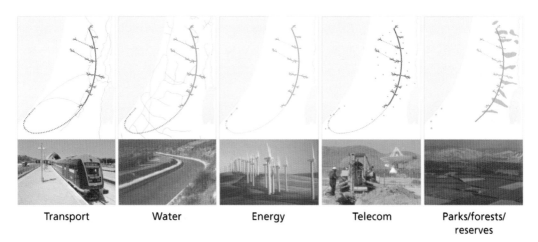

| Transport | Water | Energy | Telecom | Parks/forests/reserves |

The Arc is the proposed trunk line of the Palestinian national infrastructure corridor, linking Gaza and the West Bank. It includes the rapid rail line, a national water carrier, energy generation and transmission, telecommunications lines, and a national linear park. Each of the infrastructures has east-west lateral branches that create the framework for linear development in each urban area and the boundaries for the national open space system of parks, forests, reserves, and farmlands.

opment goals, we suggest the creation of a toll road with fewer rather than more lanes and with very limited exit and entry points, perhaps one or two for each urban center.

An international airport connecting Palestine to the rest of the world is also assumed to be of critical importance in building both the identity and economy of the new state. We have further assumed that for reasons of security, the major Palestinian airport will necessarily be located in Gaza, rather than the West Bank. A parallel need will be for an international seaport, located south of Gaza City. The Arc's rail and road links will provide rapid access for passengers and freight to and from the airports and seaports for all parts of Palestine.

Finally, while the transportation infrastructure of the Arc is initially intended to address internal linkages, it can ultimately provide the backbone for land travel and transport between the international capitals of Amman, Beirut, Cairo, and Damascus—and eventually Haifa, Tel Aviv, and Be'er Sheva. International points of entry would be found at Jenin, Tulkarem, Qalqilya, south of Hebron, and east of Jericho. Infrastructure investment could be focused on linking these perimeters to the trunk of the Arc.

Fostering "Linear" Growth

Conventional practice would locate each new station along the Arc in the historic center of each existing city. However, the Arc concept intentionally sets each station area at a considerable distance—anywhere from 2 to 15 miles—from the historic center (see Figure 5). This is done for a number of reasons. First, since there is virtually no existing rail infrastructure in the Palestinian towns and cities, the costs and disruption from intruding the rights-of-way and infrastructure needed for intercity rail would be unacceptably high. Second, the presence of the station in the middle of the existing center would encourage greater concentrations and crowding in settings that are already fairly well built up; the pressure to destroy historic buildings and precincts in order to build denser and higher would only grow with time. Third, a station in the historic center would create pressure for radial growth around the center, creating ever greater problems of access from periphery to center as the city enlarges. By contrast, the proposed remote location of the station encourages a regulated, linear form of expansion from the historic center along a new artery equipped with public transit designed to meet the demands of long-term growth.

A perennial problem for developing countries in particular is the tendency toward excessive centralization—for one urban area to become a mega-city that drains investment and economic growth from all other urban centers. One of the goals of the Arc concept is to minimize the differences between the different cities in order to encourage investment and growth more equitably along the line of the Arc and therefore throughout the West Bank and Gaza.

The strategy of locating the new station area at a distance from the historic core is predicated on the construction of a new connective boulevard system between them (see Figure 6). The boulevard may be a single roadway or a hierarchical system of parallel paths of different size and function. The boulevard structure organizes the growth from the historic core toward the station, since in the short term the core is likely to swell, even overcrowd, as the first wave of refugees returns. Pressure to expand can be directed along the sides of the boulevard, where new neighborhoods can be developed.

The Arc concept offers the promise of a system of national open space that could be developed by merging two existing environmental systems: the extensive landscape of agricultural fields, terraces, groves, and the farms and villages associated with them and the collection of protected forests and nature preserves already designated throughout the West Bank. The particular character and uses of open space would require careful study, but conceptually, it ought to be possible to take a brief walk or bike ride along the linear park within the metropolitan area of, say, Nablus or Bethlehem; or, more ambitiously, to undertake a hike or ride along the full extent of the Arc.

Figure 5
A Ladder of Linear Cities

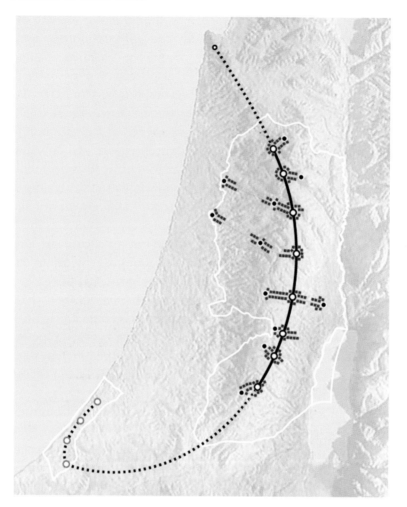

Each rail station along the Arc is strategically sited to create an east-west line of urban growth between the historic center and the new station area. The line between the two poles is established with the construction of a transit boulevard (typically from 5 to 15 kilometers in length) served primarily by rapid bus transit and taxis. Along the boulevard, new neighborhoods can be developed sequentially to accommodate as many as 3 million people in the next 15 years. The pattern creates the locations—and the boundaries—for long-term urban growth, assuring protection of the national open space system.

Figure 6
Aerial View of "Arc"

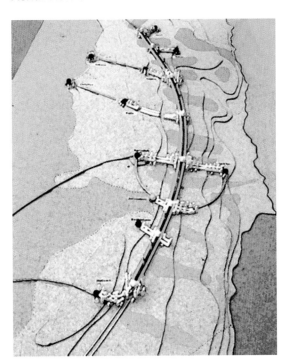

Aerial view showing the Arc within the West Bank, including the infrastructure trunk lines, the lateral boulevards or "branches" between the new station areas (white dots) and historic centers (black dots), and the parks and reserves of the national open space system.

New Neighborhoods

At the heart of the Arc concept is the settling of several million people in new neighborhoods along the flanks of the new transit boulevards. Here the sequential, ongoing creation of new neighborhoods can be calibrated to the pace of population growth and refugee return.

In addition to housing, the new neighborhoods would include shops, markets, schools, clinics, mosques and other religious structures, small parks, and cultural facilities (see Figure 7). Typical building heights might range from two to six stories. These neighborhoods can extend away from the boulevard for some distance, typically up the slopes of the defining hillsides. This distance should not be more than 3/4 of a mile—or a 15-minute walk—from the boulevard in order to encourage tran-

Figure 7
Aerial View of Prototypical Municipal Area

Aerial view showing a prototypical municipal growth pattern along the transit boulevard (blue), starting from the historic center (upper left) and extending to the new station area (lower right). Also visible are historic Route 60 (along the top), and the new
rail, water, energy, road, and park infrastructure along the line of the Arc.

sit use and discourage dependence on the automobile. Jobs should be found at virtually all points along the boulevard, although the nature of the jobs will vary from district to district.

Along the connecting boulevards themselves, uses could include newer housing,
commercial areas, office buildings, midsize hotels, government agencies, consulates,
schools, and cultural facilities. Buildings would probably be taller than in the neighborhoods behind and might include mid-rise elevator buildings or even, where ap-
propriate, high-rise buildings. Typical heights might be from five to ten stories.

Based on a very preliminary review, it is our belief that there is sufficient
buildable terrain for a boulevard between each of the new stations and historic centers to accommodate the two million new residents at the proposed average density
of 30,000 people per square mile. Another one million new residents would be
housed through increased density in the built-up areas around the core and/or
through some voluntary location in the smaller towns.

It should be stressed that while these numbers reflect demographic estimates
through 2020, the Arc is intended to create a framework that can absorb Palestinian

population growth and urban development over the long term. The combined tactics of urban density, public transit, and protected open space should be capable of supporting a sustainable, livable environment for generations.

Costs and Direct Economic Benefits of Constructing the Arc

As with the development options described in *Building a Successful Palestinian State,* the construction of the key elements of the Arc will require very substantial investment of economic resources. At the same time, the employment associated with such major infrastructure development projects is important in its own right, in addition to the longer-term economic and social benefits of these projects.

We focus on construction costs in two areas: transportation—specifically a railroad and highway along the main length of the Arc, "boulevard" roads connecting the historical population centers to the train stations located on the Arc, the train stations themselves, and transit stations along the boulevard roads—and housing—for immigrants to a new Palestinian state. For reasons we discuss in *The Arc: A Formal Structure for a Palestinian State,* the cost estimates exclude the cost of land acquisition, whether for roads, railways, stations, or housing. All costs are reported in nominal (i.e., current-year) U.S. dollars.

We estimate that construction of the main sections of the Arc railway, from Tulkarm in the north to Gaza in the south, to be approximately $3.3 billion, including rolling stock. The main highway along the Arc would cost approximately $2.1 billion, while construction of the connecting boulevard roads would be approximately $275 million. Construction of the main rail and road stations on the Arc and the smaller stations along the connecting boulevard roads would be approximately $300 million. Thus we estimate the total costs of the core rail and road infrastructure of the Arc to be around $6 billion.

With respect to housing costs, we assumed that most Palestinians will rely on their own efforts and resources to build or improve housing. At the same time, we recognize that a substantial influx of immigrants may have sufficiently large effects on local housing markets that donors may want to mitigate these effects. We therefore include an estimate of the costs of constructing new housing for returnees. Assuming the same density of residents per dwelling as currently exist in Gaza and the West Bank (6.4 people per unit) and our working estimate of 630,000 new immigrants over ten years, an additional 100,000 housing units would be needed to house this influx. At an estimated average cost of $25,000 per housing unit, this totals $2.5 billion.

The construction of transportation infrastructure and housing would employ Palestinian construction workers, increasing employment and family incomes. We have estimated the potential number of construction jobs generated by this spending by dividing the total value of projected construction spending in dollars by an estimate of gross construction output per worker in dollars derived from employment and national income accounting statistics from neighboring Arab states. Based on a total investment of $8.5 billion, roughly 530,000 person years of construction labor would be needed to complete the projects described here, based on Jordanian data. Using analogous data for Egypt, where labor productivity in construction is lower than in Jordan, we estimate that employment would run 800,000 person years. Assuming that the main Arc projects would be built over a five-year time span, we thus estimate that the necessary level of financial investment would employ 100,000 to 160,000 Palestinians per year over this period.

We emphasize that these cost and employment estimates are approximate. We intend them as a frame of reference for considering the scale of financial assistance that will be required from the international community to help develop a successful Palestinian state. More-precise estimates will require formal cost studies involving detailed needs assessments. Moreover, neither of the RAND reports discussed here includes the costs of all the major institutional changes and improvements in infrastructure that would be required for a successful Palestinian state.

Social and Political Challenges of Absorbing Refugees

As we have described, the Arc concept was designed to help address the physical and economic needs of the Palestinian population, now and in the future, without particular regard to whether population growth is due to natural increase or to immigration of refugees. At the same time, it is clear that the absorption of large numbers of immigrants will challenge a new Palestinian state in ways that go beyond the physical accommodation of additional residents, and there is considerable value to considering these challenges explicitly.

As part of the Arc project, we therefore consider a series of important social, political, and economic challenges that the Palestinian state will face as it addresses the issue of absorbing substantial numbers of new immigrants, who are likely to come principally from the Palestinian refugee communities in Lebanon, Syria, and Jordan.

The most basic challenge will eventuate in the form of a series of dilemmas:

- The legitimacy of the new government will depend in part on its success in resettling the bulk of Palestinian refugees. Yet the influx of a large number of refugees will strain the institutions of the state in a way that will challenge its ability to provide good governance, and thus its legitimacy.
- Moreover, a government striving to establish its legitimacy may have to ask the current nonrefugee population of Palestine to accept minority status once large numbers of returning refugees join the current refugee population.

- The new government will have an interest in ensuring social cohesion at the national level, which calls for dispersing returnees in a way that does not perpetuate societal cleavages. Yet returnees will want to settle where their families are already located and might oppose a government that seeks to disperse them.
- The new government may not be able to confine its resettlement efforts to refugees returning from abroad. The large number of refugees that have been living in camps within Palestine for several generations, plus the many displaced persons, who are all but refugees without the legal title, are likely to demand equal treatment. This will burden the new government with even greater responsibilities.
- Finally, the new government will have to overcome the deep skepticism that returnees from Lebanon, Jordan, and Syria harbor toward state authority, even as they must wean these communities from their dependence on the state.

In practice, it was outside the scope of the present analysis to develop detailed policy options to address all of these issues. Moreover, the social and political nature of these issues means that they are best addressed locally, in ways that reflect national preferences and the realities of the settlement terms under which an independent Palestinian state is created. At the same time, we think that the detailed consideration of these issues that we provide in *The Arc: A Formal Structure for a Palestinian State* will help stimulate discussion and planning about these issues, so that they can be addressed rapidly and effectively as circumstances require.

CHAPTER FOUR

Conclusion

Achieving Successful Development

If a state of Palestine is created, it is essential that it succeed. The purpose of RAND's analysis is to describe steps that Palestinians, Israelis, Americans, and the international community can take to ensure that a new independent Palestinian state is successful.

An independent Palestinian state will begin with many strengths. These include a population that is devoted to the success of their state and, according to polls, willing to live side by side and in peace with Israel. This population is relatively healthy and well-educated, compared with those of other countries in the region with similar levels of economic development; moreover, both the health and education infrastructures have proven themselves to be flexible and adaptive, even in the face of severe social, political, and economic strain. Particularly notable is the strong degree of gender parity in education outcomes. In health, education, and other areas, a Palestinian state will be able to draw on a strong base of governmental and nongovernmental institutions and on many highly qualified professionals.

At the same time, the new state will face significant challenges. Most fundamentally, the state must achieve security within its borders, provide for the routine safety of its inhabitants, be free from radical subversion or foreign exploitation, and pose no security threat to Israel—conditions that have been lacking since at least the start of the second intifada in 2000. The state must establish and maintain effective governance, rather than the corrupt and authoritarian rule that has prevailed since 1994. The state will have a large and rapidly growing population, with a very high dependency ratio (i.e., the ratio of children and elders to workers) and the likely immigration of large numbers of Palestinians from abroad; and it will start with a physical infrastructure that is inadequate to meet the needs of its current population, let alone accommodate a large number of returning refugees. And Palestine will face the tremendous challenge of achieving substantial and sustained economic growth.

In our view, the implementation of policies and programs along the lines of those recommended in *Building a Successful Palestinian State* and *The Arc: A Formal Structure for a Palestinian State* is necessary, if insufficient, for the success of an independent Palestinian state over its first decade. Such implementation, in turn, will require strong political and financial commitments from the international community.

As a frame of reference for the magnitude of funding that may be required from international donors to ensure successful Palestinian development, we considered the cases of Bosnia and Kosovo, two areas where the international community has recently invested very large sums for post-conflict reconstruction. Like the West Bank and Gaza, these two entities suffered considerable damage from conflicts. Both Bosnia and Kosovo have attracted considerable international interest and assistance; and both have had some success in creating democratic governments and revitalizing the local economies.

In the chapter on economic development in *Building a Successful Palestinian State*, we describe scenarios of economic growth that assume levels of capital investment of around $3.3 billion per year, or some $33 billion over the first decade of independence (this would include most or all of the specific investment needs we describe in our analyses). In per-capita terms, this represents an annual average of approximately $760 per person. For comparison, this represents about 2.5 times the amount of international aid per capita provided to the West Bank and Gaza in 2002 (approximately $300), less than twice the per-capita amount provided to Kosovo in the first two post-conflict years ($433), and only slightly more than the per-capita amount provided to Bosnia in its first two post-conflict years ($714).

Thus there are recent precedents for providing levels of international aid per capita that approach what we estimate will be needed in Palestine. At the same time, the level of international commitment we describe is higher (in per-capita and absolute terms) and is sustained over a longer period of time than the assistance provided to Bosnia, Kosovo, or other major international aid efforts in recent times. Achieving this commitment will require concerted international cooperation.

Looking to the Future

At the time of this writing, the prospects for establishing an independent Palestinian state are uncertain. U.S. attention, without which a negotiated settlement between Palestinians and Israelis seems unlikely, has been focused primarily on Iraq. Nevertheless, a critical mass of Palestinians and Israelis—as well as the United States, Russia, the European Union, and the United Nations—remains committed to the goal of establishing a Palestinian state. And recent events, including the death of Yasser Arafat and the election of Mahmoud Abbas as his replacement, may yet turn this eventuality into a more imminent reality.

Our analyses are motivated by a firm belief that thoughtful preparation can facilitate peace. Certainly, when peace comes, such preparation will be essential to the success of the new state, as recent U.S. experience in Iraq and Afghanistan helps illustrate. Our work is designed to help Palestinians, Israelis, and the international community prepare for the moment when the parties are ready to create and sustain a successful Palestinian state.

مساعدة دولة فلسطينية على النجاح
النتائج الرئيسية

يستند هذا المجلد إلى الدراسات التالية:

بناء دولة فلسطينية ناجحة

مدراء المجموعات الدراسية

ستيفن ن. سايمون، ك. روس أنثوني، غلان ي. روبنسون، ديفيد ك. غومبرت، جيرولد د. غرين، روبرت ي. هانتر، ك. ريتشارد نو، كينيث ا. شاين.

المؤلفون

دجاستن ل. أدمز، عادل ق. عفيفي، ك. روس أنثوني، شيريل بينارد، مارك بيرنستين، ديفيد برانان، ريتشل كريستينا، سينثيا ر. كوك، كيث كرين، ريتشارد ج. دكلبوم، كاتيرينا فونكيش، تشارلز ا. غولدمان، ديفيد ج. غروفز، سيث ج. جونز، كيفين ف. مكارثي، أمبر مورين، براين نيكيبوراك، كيفن جاك رايلي، غلان ا. روبنسون، مايكل شونبوم، ستيفن ن. سايمون، أنغا ر. تيميلسينا.

القوس: بنية منهجية لدولة فلسطينية

المؤلفون

دوغ سويسمان، ستيفان ن. سايمون، غلان ا. روبنسون، ك. روس أنثوني، مايكل شونبوم

الدعم المالي من هبة السيد ديفيد والسيدة كارول ريتشاردز وهبة أخرى من السيد غيلفورد غليزر، ومن خلال هبات، من عديد من الأفراد، ومن خلال الدخل المتوفر من بحوث يمولها عملاء المؤسسة.

التمويل الأساسي للبحث الموصوف في هذا التقرير مقدم من أشخاص فرديين. أما التمويل لــ"بناء دولة فلسطينية ناجحة" [Building a Successful Palestinian State]، فكان هبة من السيد ديفيد والسيدة كارول ريتشاردز، بينما بادر السيد غيلفورد غليزر بــ"القوس: بنية منهجية لدولة فلسطينية" [The Arc: A Formal Structure for a Palestinian State] التي تم تمويلها بواسطة هبة كريمة منه. ولقد حظى أيضاً هذا البحث الذي أجري من أجل المصلحة العامة بدعم من مؤسسة راند عن طريق هبات من عديد من الأفراد وُضعت في تصرف مؤسسة راند، ومن خلال الدخل المتوفر من بحوث عملاء المؤسسة.

بيانات فهرسة منشورات مكتبة الكونغرس متوفرة لهذا المنشور

ISBN 0-8330-3771-4

الغلاف تصميم Ph.D، www.phdla.com
صورة الخلفية: مجلة الصلاح. صورة الكوة: (الثلاثة الأولى): الصور إهداء بيري فيدال إي دومينيتش؛ (أقصى اليمين): "شجرة الزيتون: مرحباً ماما، أنا وصلت!" الصورة إهداء ستيف سابيلا على
www.sabellaphoto.com
الرسوم والصور على الصفحات ١٦ و٢١ حتى ٢٣ و٢٥ و٢٦ إهداء شركة Suisman Urban Design

منشور مؤسسة راند لعام ٢٠٠٥
1776 Main Street, P.O. Box 2138, Santa Monica, CA 90407-2138
1200 South Hayes Street, Arlington, VA 22202-5050
201 North Craig Street, Suite 202, Pittsburgh, PA 15213-1516
موقع مؤسسة راند على الانترنت: http://www.rand.org/
لطلب مستندات مؤسسة راند أو للحصول على المزيد من المعلومات، اتصل بخدمات التوزيع على: الهاتف: ٧٠٠٢-٤٥١ (٣١٠)؛ الفاكس: ٦٩١٥-٤٥١ (٣١٠)؛ البريد الالكتروني: order@rand.org

تمهيد

تؤيد كل من السلطة الفلسطينية وإسرائيل والولايات المتحدة والاتحاد الأوروبي وروسيا والأمم المتحدة كلها رسمياً إنشاء دولة فلسطينية مستقلة. ومنذ وفاة ياسر عرفات والانتخابات التي جرت في الآونة الأخيرة في قطاع غزة والضفة الغربية، نشأ إهتمام في أوساط عديدة في إعادة إحياء عملية السلام.

يلخص هذا المستند البحث الذي أجرته مؤسسة راند [RAND Corporation] لوضع توصيات مبنية على تحليل دقيق جداً للخطوات التي قد يتخذها الفلسطينيون وإسرائيل والولايات المتحدة والمجموعة الدولية لتعزيز نجاح الدولة في حال إنشاء دولة فلسطينية. ونتائج هذا البحث مفصّلة في منشورين منفصلين: "بناء دولة فلسطينية ناجحة" [*Building a Successful Palestinian State*] و"القوس: بنية منهجية لدولة فلسطينية" [*The Arc: A Formal Structure for a Palestinian State*]. كما ويبحث تقرير مرافق سيصدر قريباً بعنوان "بناء دولة فلسطينية ناجحة: الأمن" [*Building a Successful Palestinian State: Security*] القضايا الأمنية بالمزيد من التفاصيل.

في الدراستين الأولتين، وضعت مؤسسة راند تقديرات أولية لتكاليف تنفيذ توصياتها. والتقديرات الملخصة في نهاية هذا المستند للتمويل اللازم لتنفيذ توصيات مؤسسة راند يقع ضمن إمكانيات الموارد الدولية والمستثمرين الفرديين. وبالرغم من أن تحاليل مؤسسة راند تفترض وجود معاهدة سلام، إلا أن العديد من التوصيات في كلا الدراستين يمكن تنفيذها فوراً.

إن هذا البحث جدير باهتمام المجتمعات الفلسطينية والإسرائيلية؛ ومسؤولي الحكومة الفلسطينية؛ وواضعي السياسات في "رباعي خريطة الطريق" (الولايات المتحدة والإتحاد الأوروبي والأمم المتحدة وروسيا)؛ وخبراء السياسة الخارجية؛ والهيئات والأفراد الملتزمين بالمساعدة على إنشاء دولة ناجحة في فلسطين وإدامتها. ويجب أيضاً أن يحظى باهتمام الفرق المتفاوضة المنوطة بمسؤولية إنشاء الدولة الجديدة.

لقد أجري البحث الأساسي لهاتين الدراستين من أيلول ٢٠٠٢ حتى أيلول ٢٠٠٤ من قبل فرق متعددة التخصصات من باحثي مؤسسة راند العاملين بإدارة "مركز راند الصحي للأمن الصحي المحلي والدولي" [RAND Health Center for Domestic and International Health Security] و"مركز السياسة العامة في الشرق الأوسط" [Center for Middle East]

Public Policy أو [CMEPP، وهو أحد البرامج الدولية لمؤسسة راند. والمركزان تابعان لمؤسسة راند.

التمويل الأساسي لكل من هذه الدراسات توفر من هبات سخية فردية. فتمويل دراسة "بناء دولة فلسطينية ناجحة" [Building a Successful Palestinian State] تم بفضل هبة من السيد ديفيد والسيدة كارول ريتشاردز، بينما تمت دراسة "القوس: بنية منهجية لدولة فلسطينية" [The Arc: A Formal Structure for a Palestinian State] بمبادرة وهبة من السيد غيلفورد غليزر. كما ان هذا البحث من أجل المصلحة العامة حظي بدعم مادي من خلال هبات من عديد من الأفراد وُضعت في تصرف مؤسسة راند، ومن خلال الدخل المتوفر من بحوث يمولها عملاء المؤسسة.

المحتويات

الفصل الثالث

الرسوم

المقدمة

من أيلول ٢٠٠٢ حتى أيلول ٢٠٠٤، أجرت مؤسسة راند دراستين ركزتا على السؤال حول كيفية التمكن من إنجاح دولة فلسطينية مستقلة.

عاينت الدراسة الأولى مجموعة واسعة من التحديات السياسية والاقتصادية والاجتماعية والبيئية التي قد تواجهها دولة فلسطينية حديثة، من أجل التعرف على الخيارات التي يستطيع الفلسطينيون والإسرائيليون والمجموعة الدولية تبنيها لتعزيز فرص نجاح هذه الدولة. واعتمدت دراستنا الثانية على الدراسة الأولى لمؤسسة راند لتبحث في خيارات تلبية احتياجات العدد المتزايد للسكان الفلسطينيين من حيث الإسكان والنقل والبنى التحتية. وتبحث الدراسة الثانية جلياً في القضايا المتعلقة بالعودة المحتملة لعدد طائل من اللاجئين الفلسطينيين إلى دولة فلسطينية جديدة.

تمثل هذه الخلاصة التنفيذية أبرز وقائع الدراستين. وعلى القراء الباحثين عن المزيد من المعلومات الاستعانة بالتقريرين التاليين:

RAND Corporation, Palestinian State Study Group (Steven N. Simon, C. Ross Anthony, Glenn E. Robinson et al.), *Building a Successful Palestinian State,* Santa Monica, Calif.: The RAND Corporation, MG-146-DCR, 2005.

Doug Suisman, Steven N. Simon, Glenn E. Robinson, C. Ross Anthony, and Michael Schoenbaum, *The Arc: A Formal Structure for a Palestinian State,* Santa Monica, Calif.: RAND Corporation, MG-327-GG, 2005.

الفصل الثاني
بناء دولة فلسطينية ناجحة

إن التعرف على متطلبات النجاح هو حاجة سياسية ملحة في حال إنشاء دولة فلسطينية جديدة. ولا تزال مجموعة حاسمة من الفلسطينيين والإسرائيليين، بالإضافة إلى الولايات المتحدة وروسيا والاتحاد الأوروبي والأمم المتحدة، ملتزمة بإنشاء دولة فلسطينية. إن مبادرة "خريطة الطريق" التي حظت بمصادقة رسمية من كافة هذه الأطراف، كانت قد دعت إلى إنشاء دولة فلسطينية جديدة بحلول سنة ٢٠٠٥.[١] ولقد قام الرئيس الأميركي بوش في الآونة الأخيرة بتعديل هذا الجدول الزمني للولايات المتحدة، داعياً إلى دولة جديدة بحلول سنة ٢٠٠٩. وبالرغم من أن امكانيات إنشاء دولة فلسطينية مستقلة لا تزال غير أكيدة، إلا أن التاريخ الحديث في بناء الدول يشير جلياً إلى أن مثل هذه الجهود تفشل تقريباً دائماً في غياب خطط مفصلة.

لقد بحثت مؤسسة راند في خيارات لهيكلة مؤسسات دولة فلسطينية مستقبلية من أجل تعزيز فرص نجاح الدولة. ولم نبحث في كيفية تمكن الأطراف من التوصل إلى تسوية قد تنشيء دولة فلسطينية مستقلة، بل وضعنا توصيات مبنية على تحليل موضوعي ومتعلقة بالخطوات التي يستطيع الفلسطينيون وإسرائيل والولايات المتحدة والمجموعة الدولية إتخاذها الآن، وعند إنشاء دولة فلسطينية مستقلة، لزيادة احتمال نجاح الدولة الجديدة.

إن عملية بناء دولة هي صعبة جداً حتى في ظل ظروف تمثل تحديات أقل. وحتى لو تم الاتفاق على السلام، سيبقى عدم الثقة كبيراً بين الفلسطينيين والإسرائيليين، ومن المرجح أن يحاول المنشقون في البلدين ومن الخارج أن يعرقلوا التقدم نحو دولة فلسطينية ناجحة. وسيتطلب النجاح التخطيط الجيد؛ والموارد الطائلة؛ والثبات؛ والمشاركة الكبيرة والمستمرة للمجموعة الدولية؛ والبسالة والإلتزام والعمل الجاهد من جانب الشعب الفلسطيني.

---

[١] إن العنوان الكامل لخريطة الطريق هو: *A Performance-Based Roadmap to a Permanent Two-State Solution to the Israeli-Palestinian Conflict* ويمكن الاطلاع عليها على http://www.state.gov/r/pa/ei/rls/22520.htm إعتباراً من شباط ٢٠٠٥.

الأسلوب

بحثنا في المرحلة الأولى من تحليلنا في أسس دولة جديدة ناجحة، خصوصاً طبيعة المؤسسات التي ستحكمها والهياكل والعمليات التي ستحافظ على الأمن. ثم قدمنا وصفاً للموارد الديموغرافية والاقتصادية والبيئية التي تستطيع الدولة الفلسطينية الاعتماد عليها، والعوامل التي قد تحد من قدرة الدولة على استعمال تلك الموارد بفعالية. أخيراً، بحثنا في ما يجب أن تقوم به الدولة الفلسطينية لتضمن عافية مواطنيها وتعليمهم.

وفي كل من هذه المجالات، اعتمدنا على أفضل المعلومات التجريبية المتوفرة لوصف متطلبات النجاح، وللتعرف على السياسات البديلة لتلبية هذه المتطلبات، ولتحليل عواقب اختيار بدائل أخرى. وبالنسبة لمعظم المجالات، وضعنا أيضاً تقديراً للتكاليف المالية المرتبطة بتنفيذ توصياتنا خلال العقد الأول من الاستقلال. والتكاليف مقدمة بالسعر الثابت للدولار الأميركي لعام ٢٠٠٣، بدون أي محاولة لتعديل التقديرات للاتجاهات المستقبلية في التضخم أو في أسعار صرف العملات. واختلفت وسيلة احتساب التكاليف وفقاً لطبيعة الأسئلة التحليلية وتوفر المعلومات.

إن هذه التقديرات ليست مبنية على تحاليل مفصلة للتكاليف، بل هي مقياس للمساعدة المالية التي ستكون مطلوبة من المجموعة الدولية للمساعدة في تطوير دولة فلسطينية ناجحة. وستتطلب التقديرات الأكثر دقة دراسات منهجية للتكاليف تشمل تقييمات مفصلة للاحتياجات. كما ولم نخمن تكاليف كافة التغييرات المؤسسية والتحسينات الكبرى في البنى التحتية التي ستكون مطلوبة لدولة فلسطينية ناجحة.

تعريف النجاح

برأينا سيتطلب "النجاح" في فلسطين دولة مستقلة ديموقراطية ذات حكومة فعالة تعمل في ظل سيادة القانون في بيئة سالمة وآمنة توفر متطلبات التنمية الاقتصادية وتولي دعمها للخدمات الملائمة للإسكان والتغذية والتعليم والصحة والخدمات العامة لشعبها. ولتحقيق هذا النجاح، على فلسطين أن تعالج أربعة تحديات أساسية:

- **الأمن:** يجب أن يحسن إنشاء الدولة الفلسطينية مستوى الأمن للفلسطينيين والإسرائيليين والمنطقة.

- **الحاكمية:** يجب أن تحكم الدولة الفلسطينية بفعالية وأن يقر كل من مواطنيها والمجموعة الدولية بشرعيتها.

- **التنمية الاقتصادية:** يجب أن تكون فلسطين قابلة للنمو من الناحية الاقتصادية، ومعتمدة على نفسها مع مرور الزمن.

- **رفاهة شعبها:** يجب أن تكون فلسطين قادرة على تقديم الغذاء واللباس والتعليم لشعبها، وعلى توفير احتياجاتهم الصحية والاجتماعية.

شروط النجاح

الأمن

لا يمكن تصور نجاح دولة فلسطينية مستقلة في غياب السلام والأمن للفلسطينيين والإسرائيليين على حد سواء. إن استتباب الأمن هو شرط أساسي لتحقيق كافة التوصيات الأخرى الناشئة عن تحليلنا. فالدولة الفلسطينية المستقلة يجب أن تكون آمنة داخل حدودها، وأن توفر السلامة الاعتيادية لسكانها، وأن تخلو من أعمال التخريب أو الاستغلال الأجنبي، وألا تشكل أي خطر على إسرائيل. وعلاوةً على ذلك، يجب ترسيخ هذه الشروط فور الاستقلال: فخلافاً للبنية التحية أو الصناعة، فالأمن لا يُبنى تدريجياً.

تتراوح التدابير الأمنية الناجحة من حماية الحدود المحيطة بالدولة إلى الحفاظ على القانون والنظام داخلها. وحتى في أفضل الظروف، سيتطلب النجاح ربما مساعدة دولية شاملة وتعاوناً وثيقاً بين العناصر الأمنية.

الحاكمية

الحاكمية الجيدة ستكون مقياساً أساسياً لنجاح الدولة الجديدة. ومن وجهة نظرنا يجب أن تشمل تلك الحاكمية إرادة الشعب، وتمارس سيادة القانون، وتخلو فعلياً من الفساد. ويجب أن تتمتع أيضاً بدعم الشعب. ولكي تحظى الدولة الجديدة بذلك الدعم، يجب أن تكون شرعية في نظر الفلسطينيين وأن تمارس الحكم الجيد اللازم للحفاظ على احترام الشعب وتأييده. والدقة في طريقة إنشاء المؤسسات والعمليات الديموقراطية، بما فيها سيادة القانون، ستكون حيوية منذ البداية، وكانت أساسية حتى قبل إنشاء الدولة.

التنمية الاقتصادية

لا يمكن إعتبار الدولة الفلسطينية المستقلة ناجحة ما لا تتسنى لشعبها فرص اقتصادية ومستوى معيشة جيدة. لقد شهدت فلسطين في الماضي قيوداً على تنميتها الاقتصادية، فلقد بلغ دخلها القومي الفردي ذروته في أواخر التسعينات ليكون ضمن البلدان ذات "الدخل المتوسط المنخفض" (وفقاً لتعريف البنك الدولي). ومنذ ذلك الحين، تراجع الدخل القومي بنسبة النصف أو أكثر إثر بداية الإنتفاضة الثانية ضد إسرائيل في أيلول ٢٠٠٠. وستحتاج الدولة الفلسطينية المستقلة إلى تحسين أوضاع شعبها الاقتصادية بنفس الالحاح الذي ستحتاج إليه لتحسين الأوضاع الأمنية.

وأشار تحليلنا إلى أن نجاح فلسطين يتطلب الدعم والموارد والتأييد من المجموعة الدولية، وفي طليعتها الولايات المتحدة والاتحاد الأوروبي والأمم المتحدة والبنك الدولي وصندوق النقد الدولي. وستكون متطلبات الموارد ضخمة خلال عقد أو أكثر، إلا أن توفر مثل هذه الموارد لا يمكن افتراضه. فالتوفر المحدود للموارد يزيد من حاجة الدولة إلى تحقيق النجاح بسرعة، خصوصاً بالنسبة لهؤلاء الذين قد يوفرون رأسمال الاستثمار الخاص.

خلال مدة المساعدة الدولية، على الدولة الفلسطينية أن تستثمر في المعونات وليس فقط أن تستهلكها. وفي نهاية المطاف، سوف يقاس نجاح الدولة الفلسطينية المستقلة بقدرة اعتمادها الكبير على نفسها.

الرفاهة الاجتماعية

إن الشرط الرابع لنجاح الدولة الفلسطينية المستقلة هو أن تتحسن ظروف معيشة شعبها تحسناً جوهرياً مع مرور الزمن. ولقد اقترح مراقبون كثيرون أن خيبة الأمل من التحسن البطيء في ظروف المعيشة في ظل الإدارة الفلسطينية بعد عام ١٩٩٤، وتدهورها الحاد في بعض السنوات، قد ساهم مساهمة كبيرة في إندلاع الانتفاضة الثانية.

بالاضافة إلى شروط النجاح الموصوفة أعلاه، يجب تعزيز الجهاز الصحي والجهاز التربوي في فلسطين. وينطلق كلا الجهازين من مواطن قوة كبيرة، لكن سيحتاج كلاهما إلى تطور كبير، مما سيتطلب الحكم الفعال والنمو الاقتصادي، وكذلك المساعدة الفنية والمالية الخارجية.

في المجال الصحي، يمكن اعتبار الدولة ناجحة إذا تمكنت من تزويد مواطنيها بفرص الحصول على خدمات الرعاية الأولية والثانوية والثلاثية بينما تكون قادرة على تولي المهام الأساسية للصحة العامة التي تتولها دولة حديثة، بما في ذلك برامج تطعيم الأطفال. أما في مجال التعليم، فيجب تأمين فرص التعليم لجميع الأطفال لتمكينهم من تحقيق أفضل قدراتهم بينما يساهمون في الرفاهة الاقتصادية والاجتماعية للمجتمع.

القضايا المشتركة العامة: التواصل والإنفاذية والأمن

بيّن تحليلنا ثلاث قضايا مشتركة عامة ستؤثر تأثيراً كبيراً في احتمالات نجاح الدولة الفلسطينية:

- تواصل أراضي الدولة (باستثناء إنفصال غزة عن الضفة الغربية)
- استطاعة التنقل بحرية للأشخاص بين إسرائيل والدولة الفلسطينية المستقلة، ونشير إلى ذلك بـ"إنفاذية" الحدود
- مدى سيادة "الأمن" والسلامة العامة.

تؤثر هذه القضايا على كافة القضايا الأخرى التي تم البحث بها في تحاليل مؤسسة راند. ومن الضروري فهم كيفية ترابطها، وتأثيرها على الأهداف الرئيسية، والتوافق بينها.

تواصل الأراضي

ستعتمد الشرعية السياسية الفلسطينية وقابلية النمو الاقتصادي بقدر كبير على تواصل الأراضي. ومن المرجح أن تفشل الدولة الفلسطينية لو تكونت من مقاطعات غير متصلة. ويتطلب التطور السياسي والاجتماعي أن يتاح للفلسطينيين حرية التنقل داخل الأراضي الفلسطينية وبينها. كما تتطلب التنمية الاقتصادية الناجحة أن تكون حركة انتقال السلع داخل الأراضي الفلسطينية وبينها بأعلى درجة ممكنة من الحرية.

إنفاذية الحدود

إن إنفاذية الحدود أساسية لنمو اقتصاد الدولة الجديدة على المدى القصير. وستكون حركة الأشخاص بين إسرائيل وفلسطين حاسمة للاقتصاد الفلسطيني من خلال توفير فرص عمل وحرية وصول المنتجات والخدمات إلى سوق حيوي ونشط، ومن خلال تشجيع الاستثمار الخارجي في فلسطين، مع مراعاة التوازن بين الإنفاذية والمخاوف الأمنية لإسرائيل.

الأمن

الأمن هو شرط مسبق للنجاح في إنشاء وتطوير كافة النواحي الأخرى من الدولة الفلسطينية. وأحد الأبعاد الحاسمة للأمن هو ثقة المواطنين الفلسطينيين بالعيش في ظل سيادة القانون. والبعد الأساسي الثاني هو الحماية من العنف السياسي.

لقد استنتجنا أنه لا يمكن تحقيق أي من الشروط الكبرى للنجاح، أي الأمن والحاكمية الجيدة وقابلية نمو الاقتصاد والرفاهة الاجتماعية، إلا إذا كانت الأراضي الفلسطينية متواصلة فعلياً. ففي دولة لا تكون أراضيها متواصلة، يزيد الفقر من حدة الاستياء السياسي ويخلق وضعاً يكون فيه من الصعب الحفاظ على الأمنَ. وبالإضافة إلى ذلك، سيمثل إنقسام فلسطين إلى أجزاء عديدة تحدٍ أمنياً معقداً إذ أن عدم تواصل أراضي الدولة يعوق التنسيق بين هيئات تنفيذ القوانين؛ ويتطلب مضاعفة الامكانات المكلفة؛ ويجازف في إحداث الخصومات بين مسؤولي الأمن، كما حدث بين قطاع غزة والضفة الغربية في ظل السلطة الفلسطينية. إن الإنفاذية الواسعة للحدود أساسية للتنمية الاقتصادية لكنها تعقد الأمن تعقيداً كبيراً.

النتائج الرئيسية التي تم التوصل إليها من التحاليل

الحاكمية

ستتميز الدولة الفلسطينية الناجحة بالحاكمية الجيدة، بما في ذلك الإلتزام بالديموقراطية وسيادة القانون. وأحد الشروط المسبقة للحاكمية الجيدة هو أن يقر مواطنو الدولة بشرعية رؤسائهم. وفي نهاية المطاف، سيعتمد الدعم السياسي للدولة الجديدة وشرعيتها على مجموعة كبيرة من الشروط، بما فيها شكل الحاكمية وفعاليتها، والتنمية الاقتصادية والاجتماعية، وحجم الأراضي وتواصلها، ووضع القدس، وحرية اللاجئين في إعادة الاستيطان في فلسطين.

سيكون من الأسهل تحقيق الحاكمية الجيدة لو كانت حدود فلسطين مفتوحة، واقتصادها مزدهراً، واستيعابها للاجئين ممكناً، وأمنها مضموناً، وسنواتها الأولى مدعومة بمساعدة دولية طائلة. ولن يتم تحقيق الحاكمية الجيدة بدون الجهود الطائلة والمساعدة الدولية، ومن المرجح أن يأتي من خلال إصلاح المؤسسات والممارسات الحكومية الحالية. وعلى الأقل يجب أن تتبنى فلسطين الإجراءات التي (١) تعزز سيادة القانون، بما فيها منح الصلاحيات للقضاء، و(٢) تحول بعض السلطة من الفرع التنفيذي إلى الفرع التشريعي للحكومة الفلسطينية، و(٣) تخفض الفساد تخفيضاً كبيراً، و(٤) تحث على نظام الاستحقاق في الخدمة المدنية، و(٥) تنوط بالسلطة للمسؤولين المحليين. ويجب إتمام الدستور المؤقت الذي يقر بإرادة الشعب ويحدد جلياً صلاحيات مختلف فروع الحكومة. وأخيراً، يجب التخلص من الممارسات التعسفية والفساد اللذين اتسمت بهما ممارسات السلطة الفلسطينية في السابق.

سيترتب على تعزيز الحاكمية الفلسطينية تكاليف مالية، مثلاً لإجراء الانتخابات، ولإنشاء وتشغيل الفرع التشريعي والفرع التنفيذي للحكومة. ولم نقدر جلياً تكاليف هذه التغييرات في المؤسسات، إلا أنها مطروحة في بعض الحالات في تحليل القطاعات الأخرى.

الأمن الداخلي

ستكون من أكثر الشؤون إلحاحاً للأمن الداخلي بالنسبة للدولة الفلسطينية الحاجة إلى إخماد نشاط المنظمات المناضلة التي تشكل تهديداً خطيراً على الأمن بين الدول (من خلال الاعتداءات على إسرائيل والقوات الدولية) والأمن داخل الدولة (من خلال المعارضة العنيفة للسلطة الشرعية). ويجب وضع السلامة العامة والتنفيذ الاعتيادي للقوانين، أي تطبيق العدالة، في الطريق السليم بأسرع وقت ممكن.

سيسهل تطبيق العدالة إنبثاق قضاء مستقل ومؤسسة فعالة لتنفيذ القوانين قادرة على التحقيق في النشاطات الجنائية العامة ومكافحتها، وتأمين السلامة العامة. وسيتطلب كلا الهدفين موارد مالية لإعادة بناء دور العدل والشرطة، والمصادر القانونية، وأجهزة الكمبيوتر، والتدريب في الطب الشرعي وغيره، والأجهزة التي تحتاج إليها الشرطة لإتمام مهام دورياتها اليومية. إن برنامجاً أكثر شمولية لتعجيل عملية الإصلاح وأسرع لإحلال جو من الأمن للمواطنين الفلسطينيين، قد يتضمن نشر الشرطة الدولية، ومعاينة وتعيين القضاة والمدعين العامين وضباط الشرطة.

شأنها شأن حقلي مكافحة الإرهاب والاستخبارات، ستتطلب شروط الأمن الداخلي إعادة هيكلة الأجهزة الأمنية بما فيها أعلى المستويات من الأجهزة، والمراقبة، والتدريب، والدعم التحليلي. وبناءً على حدة التهديد الإرهابي المحلي وسرعة تطور الإمكانيات الفلسطينية في هذا المجال، قد تدعو الحاجة إلى برنامج مكثف أكثر.

إننا نقدر التكاليف العامة المتعلقة بإعادة بناء الأمن الداخلي بما لا يقل عن ٦٠٠ مليون دولار أميركي سنوياً، وما يعادل ٧٫٧ بليون دولار أميركي على مدى عشر سنوات.

الديموغرافيا

هناك نحو ٩ ملايين فلسطيني يعيش قرابة ٤٠ بالمئة منهم داخل حدود ما هو مرجح أن يصبح الدولة الفلسطينية الجديدة (الضفة الغربية وقطاع غزة). وتسجل نسبة المواليد إرتفاعاً كبيراً. وفي حال عودة الفلسطينيين المهاجرين على نطاق واسع، سينمو عدد السكان في الأراضي الفلسطينية بسرعة كبيرة في المستقبل القريب.

وسوف يحد النمو السريع في عدد السكان من قدرة الدولة على توفير الماء والصرف الصحي والنقل للمقيمين الفلسطينيين، وسيزيد من تكاليف القيام بذلك. وسيثقل ذلك كاهل الرأسمال المادي والبشري المطلوب لتوفير التعليم والرعاية الصحية والإسكان، وسيضع العبء المالي الثقيل لتمويل هذه الخدمات على فئة صغيرة من السكان في سن العمل. وستستعرض الدولة الفلسطينية أيضاً لضغوط كبيرة لتوفير الوظائف لعدد متزايد بسرعة من الشبان الذين سيدخلون اليد العاملة.

هناك إشارات واضحة على إنخفاض نسب التكاثر الفلسطينية، لكن معدل هذا الانخفاض غير أكيد. وستتزايد نسبة المواليد حتماً على المدى القصير إذ أن عدد النساء الفلسطينيات في سن الانجاب ستتزايد بأكثر من الضعف. أما على المدى الطويل، فستبدأ نسب التكاثر بالانخفاض. وسوف يعتمد معدل الانخفاض على مدى ارتفاع مستويات تعليم المرأة الفلسطينية ومشاركتها في اليد العاملة.

هناك شكوك كبيرة من عدد الجالية الفلسطينية التي قد تعود إلى الدولة الفلسطينية الجديدة. وتقدر الدائرة المركزية الفلسطينية للإحصائيات ودائرة الإحصائيات الأميركية عودة ما بين ١٠٠،٠٠٠ و ٥٠٠،٠٠٠ شخص. أما تقديراتنا المبنية على الافتراضات حول أي مجموعات من الفلسطينيين التي من المرجح أن تعود وفي ظل أي ظروف، فهي أعلى بعض الشيء. وفي نهاية المطاف، سيتوقف عدد الفلسطينيين العائدين على بنود الاتفاقية النهائية وحول التطورات الاجتماعية والسياسية والاقتصادية في الدولة الفلسطينية الجديدة. وهذه الوقائع الديموغرافية تؤثر تأثيراً كبيراً على التنمية الاقتصادية والاجتماعية المحتملة لأي دولة جديدة.

الماء

ستحتاج الدولة الفلسطينية القابلة للنمو إلى موارد كافية من الماء النظيف للاستهلاك المحلي، وللتنمية التجارية والصناعية، والزراعة. وهذه المتطلبات غير متوفرة اليوم. فالممارسات الحالية المتعلقة بإدارة شؤون المياه والنفايات والمجاري تحط من نوعية كل من السواقي والأنهر، وموارد المياه الجوفية.

تتوفر معظم المياه في فلسطين عن طريق الينابيع والآبار التي تغذيها مكامن المياه الجوفية المتقاسمة مع إسرائيل. ولا يوفر التطوير الحالي للموارد المائية إلا نحو النصف من النسبة المطلوبة من المياه المحلية للفرد حسب منظمة الصحة العالمية، ويحد ذلك من الري وإنتاج الأغذية. وبالإضافة إلى ذلك، فالاستعمال الحالي للمياه لن يستديم، فكمية الماء التي يستخرجها الفلسطينيون والاسرائيليون من معظم مكامن المياه الجوفية في المنطقة تتخطى نسبة إعادة الامتلاء الطبيعية.

إن الخيارات التي بحثنا فيها لزيادة الموارد المائية شملت زيادة استعمال المياه الجوفية التي يؤمنها تخفيض إسرائيل لاستعمالها؛ وزيادة نسبة التقاط مياه الأمطار؛ وزيادة قدرات إزالة الملح حيث لا توجد أي خيارات أخرى. ويمكن التحكم بالطلب عن طريق التطبيق الحذق لتكنولوجيات الاستعمال الفعّال للماء، ووسائل إعادة استعمال الماء، والتحسينات في البنية التحتية.

إننا نقدر كلفة قدرها أكثر من ٤,٩ بلايين دولار أميركي لتوفير الماء والصرف الصحي على مدى عقد حتى سنة ٢٠١٤. وقد يخفض التحسين في استراتيجيات إدارة شؤون الماء من هذا المبلغ بنسبة أقصاها ١,٣ بليون دولار أميركي حتى بليوني دولار أميركي.

الصحة

يبدأ النظام الصحي للدولة الفلسطينية المستقبلية على أساس متين، بما في ذلك سكان أصحاء نسبياً، وإيلاء قيمة اجتماعية عالية للصحة، وكثرة أصحاب المهن الطبية ذوي المؤهلات العالية، ووجود خطط وطنية لتنمية النظام الصحي، وقاعدة قوية من المؤسسات الحكومية وغير الحكومية.

تشمل النواحي الهامة التي تستدعي الاهتمام ضعف التنسيق والتنفيذ في نظام السياسات والبرامج عبر المناطق الجغرافية وبين القطاعات الحكومية وغير الحكومية للنظام الصحي، وكثرة المفتقرين للمؤهلات بين أعضاء الجهاز الصحي، وضعف الأنظمة للترخيص والتعليم المستمر، وضخامة العجز في ميزانيات وزارة الصحة الفلسطينية والنظام الحكومي للتأمين الصحي (المصدر الرئيسي للتأمين الصحي).

ركز تحليلنا على المؤسسات الرئيسية التي سيحتاج إليها نظام الرعاية الصحية خلال العقد الأول من إنشاء الدولة المستقلة. وبالإضافة إلى ذلك، أشرنا إلى برامج عديدة ملحة للصحة الوقائية والعلاجية.

نوصي بإعطاء الأولوية للمبادرات في مجالين:

• تكامل عملتي التخطيط للنظام الصحي وتنمية السياسات تكاملاً أوثق، مع الأخذ بالاعتبار ما يزوّده أصحاب الشأن من المؤسسات الحكومية وغير الحكومية المعنية من معلومات مجدية.

• تحسين برامج الرعاية الصحية العامة والأولية، بما فيها برنامج محدث للتحصين، وبرنامج شامل لإضافة المغذيات الدقيقة، والوقاية من الأمراض المزمنة وغير المعدية وعلاجها، وعلاج الحالات التنموية والنفسية الاجتماعية.

إننا نقدر أن النظام الصحي الفلسطيني قد يستوعب بشكل بنّاء ما بين ١٢٥ مليون دولار أميركي و١٦٠ مليون دولار أميركي سنوياً من الدعم الخارجي (الدولي) على مدى العقد الأول من الدولة المستقلة.

التعليم

يبدأ النظام التربوي للدولة الجديدة بأساس قوي، خصوصاً في مجالات الفرص والجودة والتقديم. وتشمل مواضع قوة الفرص التزاماً بتكافؤ الفرص والنجاح في تحقيق مساواة المرأة، والدعم المجتمعي القوي للتعليم، والقيادة الداعمة لكل من إنتشار النظام وإصلاحه. وتشمل مواضع القوة في مجال الجودة الاستعداد للمشاركة في إصلاح المناهج؛ والاهتمام القوي في تحسين أصول التدريس وموارده؛ والالتزام بتحسين مؤهلات ومكافأة أصحاب المهنة؛ وإعتبار المدارس مواقع هامة لتنمية مهارات الطلاب في التربية المدنية والمسؤولية الاجتماعية. ويخضع النظام لإدارة جيدة نسبياً ويتميز بامكانيات راسخة لجمع البيانات.

ومع ذلك، يواجه النظام تحديات جديرة بالذكر. ففي مجال الفرص، تشمل هذه التحديات إرتفاع مستويات سوء التغذية والتشرد والصحة السيئة؛ وعدم ملائمة المنشآت والمستلزمات؛ وانتفاء الأمن في المدارس والطرق المؤدية إليها؛ وغياب خيارات التعليم للطلاب ذوي الاحتياجات الخاصة؛ وغياب خيارات التعليم غير المنهجية للطلاب في سن الدراسة؛ وغياب فرص التعلم طوال الحياة. وفي ما يخص جودة التعليم، فالتحديات تشمل غياب الأهداف الواضحة والتوقعات؛ وضعف وثاقة الصلة لبرامج مراحل التعليم الثانوي والمهني والعالي؛ ومحدودية الأبحاث والإنماء؛ وقلة المكافأة المادية لأصحاب المهنة و"فيض" إداري متنامي؛ والصعوبة في مراقبة العمليات والنتائج. أما تقديم خدمات التعليم، فيعوقه نظام يفتقر إفتقاراً حاداً إلى الأموال ويعتمد على الجهات المانحة، كما ان البيانات المحدودة للنظام لا ترتبط بفعالية مع الإصلاح.

لقد بحث تحليلنا في وسائل تحسين الفرص والجودة والتقديم، بهدف وضع فلسطين على المدى الطويل كلاعب قوي في اقتصاد المعرفة في المنطقة. ونحن نوصي بمجموعة من النشاطات في إطار ثلاثة أهداف رئيسية للنظام على مدى السنوات العشرة التالية:

• الحفاظ على المستويات العالية الحالية للفرص، مع العمل ضمن قيود الموارد لتوسيع عمليات الالتحاق في التعليم الثانوي (خصوصاً في التعليم المهني والفني، والمسار العلمي الأكاديمي) وبرامج الطفولة المبكرة.

• تحسين الجودة بالتركيز على المعايير المنهجية المتكاملة، والتقييم، والتنمية المهنية، بدعم التخطيط طويل الأجل لاستدامة النظام.

• تحسين عملية التقديم بالعمل مع الجهات المانحة على وضع آليات تمويل منظمة ومتكاملة تسمح لإدارات المدارس التركيز على تلبية إحتياجات الطلاب.

إننا نقدر أن النظام التربوي الفلسطيني سيطلب ما بين بليون وبليون ونصف بليون دولار أميركي سنوياً خلال العقد الأول من قيام الدولة لتتيح للدولة مستوى من العمل يدعم الطموحات القومية للتنمية. (لا نميز بين الاستثمارات الممنوحة والقومية.) ونحن نعي أن مستويات الاستثمار هذه طائلة من الناحية المطلقة وبالنسبة لمستويات الانفاق التاريخية في فلسطين، (والتي كان معدلها نحو ٢٥٠ مليون دولار أميركي سنويا في السنوات ١٩٩٦ -

١٩٩٩). وتوصياتنا مبنية على المعايير الدولية للإنفاق لكل تلميذ في الأنظمة التربوية الناجحة. كما نعرض أيضاً خيارات لتخفيض التكاليف إذا أصبح من الضروري القيام بذلك.

التنمية الاقتصادية

لقد بحثنا في المسارات الممكنة للتنمية الاقتصادية في دولة فلسطينية مستقلة خلال الإطار الزمني الممتد من سنة ٢٠٠٥ حتى سنة ٢٠١٩، مع التركيز على الاحتمالات الفلسطينية لإدامة النمو في الدخل الفردي. المتطلبات الأساسية لنجاح التنمية الاقتصادية تشمل الأمن الكافي، والحكم الجيد، والأراضي الكافية والمتواصلة، وفرص الوصول المستقرة إلى موارد الطاقة والماء، وبنية تحتية ملائمة للنقل. وبالإضافة إلى المتطلبات الأساسية، هناك أربع قضايا حاسمة، وهي تكاليف المعاملات؛ والموارد، بما فيها الموارد والتمويل الداخليين والمعونة الخارجية؛ والنظام التجاري الفلسطيني؛ وفرص حصول اليد العاملة الفلسطينية على العمل في إسرائيل، وستحدد هذه القضايا كلها الظروف التي سيعمل في ظلها الاقتصاد الفلسطيني.

بما أن الموارد الطبيعية محدودة في الأراضي الفلسطينية، فستعتمد التنمية الاقتصادية بشكل حاسم على الرأسمال البشري، بالإضافة إلى تعزيز أنظمة التعليم الإبتدائي والثانوي والمهني لتمثل عربوناً أساسياً لأي نجاح اقتصادي مستقبلي. كما ان فرص وصول الفلسطينيين إلى أسواق العمل الإسرائيلية وتحرك الأشخاص والمنتجات بحرية كبيرة عبر حدود الدولة، بما فيها الحدود مع إسرائيل سوف تشكل عوامل أخرى هامة، إلا أنه من المرجح أن العلاقات الإسرائيلية الفلسطينية الهشة سوف تقيّد تحرك الفلسطينيين عبر الحدود إلى إسرائيل لبعض الوقت بعد إتفاقية للسلام.

إن الاختيارات الاستراتيجية التي يتخذها واضعو السياسات في مستهل الدولة الجديدة ستؤثر تأثيراً ملحوظاً على تنميتها الاقتصادية. والقرارات حول "التواصل الجغرافي"، أي حجم وشكل وأجزاء الدولة الفلسطينية المستقبلية، وضم المواقع أو المناطق الخاصة، والسيطرة على الأراضي والموارد، ستحدد كلها الموارد التي ستكون لدى قادة الدولة الجديدة لتعزيز النمو والسهولة التي يستطيع من خلالها الفلسطينيون التنقل والمشاركة في التجارة. والقرارات حول درجة "التكامل الاقتصادي" مع إسرائيل من حيث التجارة وحركة العمال الفلسطينيين سترسم شكل الاقتصاد الفلسطيني، ونسبة النمو الاقتصادي، والتوقعات للتوظيف.

إننا نعتقد أنه يمكن تطوير دولة فلسطينية مستقبلية ضمن حدود أربعة مخططات تحددها قرارات حول التواصل الجغرافي والتكامل الاقتصادي مع إسرائيل (المرتفع بالمقارنة مع المنخفض). ولقد قدرنا مستويات النمو الاقتصادي الذي يمكن تحقيقه في ظل كل من هذه المخططات مع اعتبار لمستويات معينة من الاستثمار الدولي. ولا عجب أن تحاليلنا تثبت القيمة التي تضيفها إلى التنمية الاقتصادية الدرجة العالية من التواصل الجغرافي والدرجة العالية من التكامل الاقتصادي مع إسرائيل. فدولة فلسطينية على درجة عالية من التواصل، أي تلك التي فيها عوائق قليلة أمام تحرك السلع والأشخاص، ستواجه تكاليف أقل للمعاملات وقاعدة أوسع للنشاطات الاقتصادية. وفي دولة فلسطينية ذات حدود مفتوحة وسياسات

للتجارة الحرة مع إسرائيل، ستتيسر للفلسطينيين فرص عمل مربحة في إسرائيل بالإضافة إلى توفر مستهلكين للمواد الأولية الفلسطينية ووسطاء لصادراتهم.

وفي ظل كل مخطط باستثناء مخطط التواصل المنخفض/التكامل المنخفض، من المرجح أن تتخطى فلسطين إجمالي دخلها القومي الفردي لعام ١٩٩٩ بحلول سنة ٢٠٠٩، وبلوغ ضعفه بحلول ٢٠١٩، إلا أن مثل هذا النمو الاقتصادي يفترض الاستثمار الكبير جداً في أسهم رأس المال الفلسطيني: بين سنتي ٢٠٠٥ و٢٠١٩، سيستلزم على القطاعين الخاص والعام الفلسطينيين والمجموعة الدولية استثمار نحو ٣٫٣ بلايين دولار أميركي سنوياً بمجموع قرابة ٣٣ بليون دولار أميركي على مدى عقد بعد الاستقلال (و٥٠ بليون بين سنتي ٢٠٠٥ و٢٠١٩).

وفي ظل أي من هذه المخططات، يجب أن تنمو الوظائف المحلية نمواً كبيراً في القطاع الخاص (ربما بمعدل سنوي يتراوح بين ١٥ و١٨ بالمئة) بين سنتي ٢٠٠٥ و٢٠٠٩ لبلوغ نسب العمالة التي شوهدت للمرة الأخيرة في صيف ٢٠٠٠. وستكون هذه النسب من العمالة ممكنة إن تمكنت المؤسسات التجارية الفلسطينية من العمل في بيئة تخلو نسبياً من القيود ومن استخدام الموارد المتاحة بدون قيود.

أشار تحليلنا أيضاً إلى عدد من السياسات حول أفضل السبل لتشجيع التنمية الاقتصادية ونمو الدخل الفردي. ويجب أن تشمل هذه السياسات جهوداً لتعزيز الإصلاح والاستثمار في البنية التحتية الفلسطينية المتعلقة بالنقل والماء والطاقة والاتصالات؛ فهذه البنية التحتية تشكل أساس أي اقتصاد فاعل. ويجب أيضاً أن تشمل جهوداً لتغذية النشاط الاقتصادي. وتشمل المجالات الهامة رعاية التجارة الحرة بين فلسطين وغيرها من الأماكن من خلال الحد الأدنى من تكاليف التجارة؛ والاشتراك مع جيران فلسطين لتنمية قطاعات معينة من الاقتصاد؛ وتوسيع فرص الحصول على رأس المال عن طريق برنامج لمناطق التنمية الصناعية والاقتصادية، وسياسات المعاملات المصرفية المحلية المقوّمة، وصندوق تأمين دولي؛ وتحسين مناخ الأعمال التجارية عن طريق زيادة الشفافية والمساءلة للحاكمية الفلسطينية.

تنفيذ هذه التوصيات

العديد من هذه التوصيات يمكن تنفيذها فوراً. وستكون كافة هذه القضايا هامة للبحث عند الاتفاق على دولة فلسطينية جديدة.

القوس: بنية منهجية لدولة فلسطينية

حللت الدراسة الأولى التي أجرتها مؤسسة راند بعنوان "بناء دولة فلسطينية ناجحة" مجموعة واسعة من التحديات السياسية والاقتصادية والاجتماعية والبيئية التي قد تواجهها دولة فلسطينية جديدة، ووصفت الخيارات السياسية في هذه المجالات لتسهيل نجاح الدولة. أما الدراسة الثانية التي أجرتها مؤسسة راند بعنوان "القوس: بنية منهجية لدولة فلسطينية"، فهي تعتمد على الدراسة الأولى وتقدم رؤية مفصلة لتعزيز البنية التحتية الفعلية لدولة فلسطينية. وهذه الرؤية مصممة لتعالج أحد التحديات الأساسية الموصوفة في الدراسة الأولى التي أجرتها مؤسسة راند، وهي تعزيز الرفاهة المادية والاقتصادية لعدد السكان المتنامي بسرعة في فلسطين من خلال توفير الفرص الملائمة للإسكان والنقل والاقتصاد.

إن عدد سكان الضفة الغربية وقطاع غزة البالغ نحو ٣,٦ ملايين نسمة يتنامى بسرعة كبيرة جداً بسبب الارتفاع في نسبة المواليد. وعلاوةً على ذلك، من المتوقع أن يزداد عدد السكان في فلسطين بشكل عام بعد الاستقلال وبوجه أكثر بسبب الهجرة. وفي التقدير المستخدم للدراسة الحالية، نقدر أن عدد السكان سينمو إلى نحو ٦,٦ ملايين بحلول ٢٠٢٠، أي نحو ٢,٤ ملايين نسمة من النمو الطبيعي للسكان، زائد صافي عودة نحو ٦٠٠,٠٠٠ لاجئ. ونتوقع أن تأتي الهجرة الرئيسية من اللاجئين الفلسطينيين المقيمين حالياً في لبنان وسوريا والأردن، لذا فإن البنية التحتية غير الملائمة حتى للاحتياجات الحالية في فلسطين ستكون مستلزمة قريباً إلى دعم ربما ضعف عدد السكان. (النزعات الديموغرافية الفلسطينية، بما فيها مسألة عودة اللاجئين، نوقشت مفصلاً في "بناء دولة فلسطينية ناجحة".)

لكل دولة وطنية شكل يميزها فوراً خارجياً من ترسيم الحدود الدولية المحيطة بها، كما أن لكل دولة شكلاً داخلياً يرسمه النمط السكني والحركي فيها بالنسبة إلى محيطها الطبيعي. إن النمط المحتمل لهذا الشكل الداخلي في دولة فلسطينية جديدة (بنية منهجية لدولة فلسطينية) هو موضوع تركيز المشروع الثاني لمؤسسة راند.

بالإضافة إلى وصف الخيارات لتطوير البنية التحتية الجغرافية لدولة فلسطينية تمكنها من تلبية احتياجات العدد المتنامي من سكانها، فإننا نأخذ بالاعتبار بعض من التحديات الاجتماعية والسياسية الرئيسية الناتجة عن عودة أعداد كبيرة من اللاجئين الفلسطينيين وغيرهم من المهاجرين المقيمين حالياً في الخارج إلى الدولة الجديدة.

شكل فلسطين

بدأنا بدراسة الأنماط الحالية للسكن في فلسطين. فالقرى والبلدات والمدن الفلسطينية موزعة بشكل غير متوازي في الضفة الغربية، بل تكاد تكون مجتمعة بكاملها تقريباً في نصفها الغربي، مما يعكس جلياً السمات السطحية والمناخ (انظر إلى الرسم ١). يقطع هذه المنطقة (الضفة الغربية) من الشمال إلى الجنوب خطاً مقوساً قليلاً، أو "قوس" من السلاسل الجبلية. يبلغ ارتفاع سلسلة الجبال في بعض المناطق أكثر من ٣،٠٠٠ قدم (٩٠٠ متر) عن سطح البحر، بينما يتراوح ارتفاع المرتفعات الاعتيادية بين ٢،٠٠٠ ـ ٢،٥٠٠ قدم (٦٠٠ و ٧٥٠ متر). وبسبب الرياح السائدة من الغرب إلى الشرق على ساحل البحر الأبيض المتوسط، تشهد الضفة الغربية نمط العواصف المتوسطي السائد في الساحل الغربي للولايات المتحدة الأميركية (من كاليفورنيا إلى جنوب افريقيا)، حيث يؤدي الارتفاع التصاعدي للجبال إلى هطول معظم الأمطار على الجهة الغربية من سلسة الجبال، مما يترك الجهة الشرقية جافة نسبياً. كما أن سلسلة الجبال هذه تضع المنحدرات الشرقية أيضاً في "ظل الرياح"، مما يجعلها أكثر جفافاً وأكثر حراً. وهذا يساعد في تعليل بقاء النمط السكاني للفلسطينيين بشكل عام في غرب الضفة الغربية التي تتميز بنسبة أعلى بكثير من معدل هطول الأمطار وبالأراضي الصالحة للزراعة وبالنسمات الباردة المنعشة التي تهب أحياناً على هذه المنطقة. والحالة الاستثنائية لهذا النمط السكاني الجديرة بالذكر هي واحة أريحا المنخفضة التي ساهمت مواردها المائية الجوفية الوافرة والميسرة في نمو بلدة قديمة على أرض حارة وقاحلة.

الرسم ١
قوس طبيعي

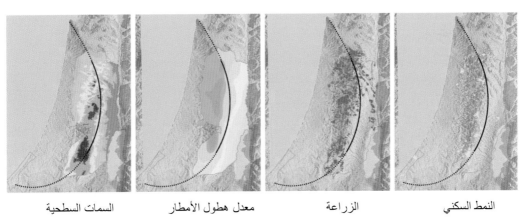

| السمات السطحية | معدل هطول الأمطار | الزراعة | النمط السكني |

يقسم الضفة الغربية في وسطها خط شمالي جنوبي مقوس قليلا أو "قوس" من السلاسل الجبلية تفصل نظام بيئة متوسطي غرباً عن المنحدرات القاحلة شرقاً. وبما أن معدل هطول الأمطار مرتفع كثيراً على الجانب الغربي، فإن الزراعة مكثفة هناك، بالإضافة إلى معظم المستوطنات الفلسطينية التاريخية.

يعرّف "أطلس فلسطين"[2] على مجموعة مؤلفة من ١١ مدينة رئيسية في الضفة الغربية. وهي من الشمال إلى الجنوب: جنين، طوباس، طولكرم، نابلس، قلقيلية، سلفيت، رام الله، أريحا، القدس، بيت لحم، والخليل. وباستثناء طولكرم وقلقيلية في الغرب وأريحا في الشرق، فإن هذه المجموعة من المدن مرتبة ترتيباً غير محكم في موازاة أو على مقربة من مسار قوس السلاسل الجبلية. وأكبر ثلاث مدن من حيث عدد السكان هي القدس (٢٥٠,٠٠٠)، والخليل (١٥٤,٠٠٠)، ونابلس (١٢٧,٠٠). أما أكبر مدينتين بعد ذلك، أي طولكرم وقلقيلية، فهما أصغر بكثير إذ يبلغ عدد سكان كل منهما أكثر بقليل من ٤٠,٠٠٠.

لقد استقر السكان في كثير من هذه المدن منذ آلاف السنين، خصوصاً الخليل، وبيت لحم، وأريحا، ونابلس. وهناك طرق قديمة تربط بينها، وفي الواقع، فإن المسار الحالي للطريق رقم ٦٠ الشمالي الجنوبي للضفة الغربية يتبع عن كثب الطريق القديم الذي كان يربط بين هذه المدن، إلا أن معظم الطريق رقم ٦٠ اليوم ضيق ومتعرج وبطيء نسبياً، مما يعكس تفضيلاً تاريخياً للسفر شمالاً على طول الطريق المسطح بمحاذاة ساحل البحر الأبيض المتوسط، وافتقاراً عاماً للاستثمار في تحديث البنية التحتية في الضفة الغربية. وتشترط التنمية الاقتصادية المستقبلية في فلسطين جلياً إنشاء مواصلات سريعة بين الشمال والجنوب للسلع والأشخاص في الضفة الغربية، وبين الضفة الغربية وقطاع غزة.

ولا يمكن اختتام البحث حول الظروف الراهنة بدون تناول مسألة المستوطنات الإسرائيلية العديدة في الضفة الغربية والطرق التي أنشئت لخدمتها. فهذه تشكل نظاماً مدينياً مستقلاً، وتختلف في مواقعها وتصميمها عن أنماط البناء التاريخية في المنطقة. ولهذه الأسباب، ولأن القرار السياسي النهائي حولها لم يتخذ، فقد اخترنا عدم التطرق إلى مسألة المستوطنات الإسرائيلية في هذا السياق.

كثافة السكان وخيارات النمو

يبلغ عدد سكان فلسطين أكثر من ٣,٦ مليون نسمة في مساحة تزيد عن ٦,٠٠٠ كيلومتر مربع (٢,٣٠٠ ميل مربع) بقليل، وبالتالي تبلغ كثافة سكانها اليوم أكثر من ٥٥٠ شخصاً في الكيلومتر المربع (١,٤٠٠ شخص في الميل المربع). وتضعها هذه الكثافة السكانية في مرتبة قريبة من أعلى البلدان كثافة في العالم. فأكثر البلدان كثافة في أوروبا هي هولندا التي تبلغ كثافة السكان فيها ٤٥٠ شخص في الكيلومتر المربع (١,٢٠٠ شخص في الميل المربع)، بينما تبلغ الكثافة السكانية في إسرائيل ٣٠٠ شخص في الكيلومتر المربع (٧٧٠ شخصاً في الميل المربع) وفي لبنان ٣٥٠ شخصاً في الكيلومتر المربع (٨٧٠ في الميل المربع). وتبلغ الكثافة السكانية في البلد ذات أعلى كثافة سكانية في العالم وهي بنغلادش ٨٥٠ شخصاً في الكيلومتر المربع (٢,٢٠٠ شخص في الميل المربع). وإذا ازداد عدد سكان فلسطين كما هو متوقع ليبلغ أكثر من ٦ ملايين خلال السنوات الـ١٥ التالية، فستبلغ كثافتها السكانية ٩٠٠

---

٢ "أطلس فلسطين" [Atlas of Palestine]، القدس (بيت لحم): معهد الأبحاث التطبيقية، ٢٠٠٢.

شخص في الكيلومتر المربع (٢,٤٠٠ شخص في الميل المربع) لتتخطى كثافة السكان في بنغلادش.

غالباً ما يتزامن ارتفاع كثافة السكان باكتظاظ السكان والفقر والمرض وازدحام السير وفقدان الحيوية الاقتصادية، وانحطاط البيئة، إلا أن ارتفاع كثافة السكان بحد نفسه ليس بالضرورة فرض للفشل على المستوى القومي. فهناك نوع من العلاقة العكسية عند مقارنة كثافة المدن مع كثافة الدول. ويشير عدد متزايد من الأبحاث والأفكار إلى أنه إذا توفرت بعض الحالات، أي الاستدامة، أداء البيئة، وانخفاض استهلاك الطاقة، قابلية العيش، والمساواة الاجتماعية، فإن المدن ذات الكثافات السكانية العالية قد يفوق أداؤها عن تلك ذات الكثافات السكانية الأدنى.

بينما تسجل مدن عديدة في الولايات المتحدة وأستراليا مثل هيوستن وفينكس وأديليد وبريزبن معدل كثافات سكانية في المدن تبلغ نحو ١,١٥٠ شخص في الكيلومتر المربع (٣,٠٠٠ شخص في الميل المربع)، فإن عدة مدن آسيوية وأوروبية مزدهرة مثل سنغافورة وباريس وميونخ تسجل كثافات لا تقل عن عشرة أضعاف، بمعدل ٣,٨٥٠ شخص في الكيلومتر المربع (٣٠,٠٠٠ في الميل المربع). إن التنمية الناجحة لتلك المدن مرتبطة بالشكل المديني المكتنز، وارتفاع الكثافة السكانية في المساكن ووسائل النقل العام الجيدة. فلو تم الجمع بين الكثافة السكانية الحالية العالية والمتوقعة لدولة فلسطينية مع أنماط معينة من التنمية المدينية والنقل العام، فقد يكون ذلك مفيداً عند البحث عن بنية منهجية للدولة قابلة للنمو.

نظراً لموقع وحجم وترابط البلدات والمدن الفلسطينية القائمة حالياً، يمكننا البحث في خيارات مختلفة لتوسيع مساحات "الاستيطان الفلسطيني" لاستيعاب الملايين من الأشخاص الإضافيين. وهناك نماذج مختلفة عديدة للتوزيع المديني للأخذ بالاعتبار، وقد اختار فريق البحث التركيز على أربعة نماذج مميزة (أنظر إلى الرسم ٢).

الرسم ٢
أربعة نماذج ممكنة لتوزيع السكان

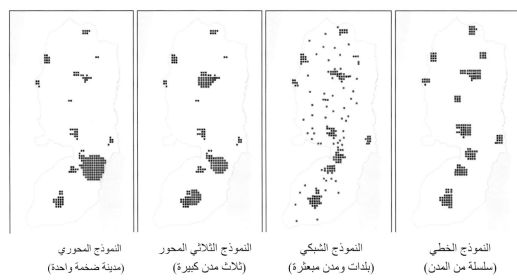

النموذج المحوري   النموذج الثلاثي المحور   النموذج الشبكي   النموذج الخطي

(مدينة ضخمة واحدة)   (ثلاث مدن كبيرة)   (بلدات ومدن مبعثرة)   (سلسلة من المدن)

تم تقييم حسنات وسيئات أربعة نماذج لتوزيع السكان. أزيل النموذجين الأولين بسبب افتقارهما إلى الأراضي المطلوبة وخطر اكتظاظ السكان. النموذج الثالث كان كثير الفوائد بشكل ولكن سجل بكلفة عالية فيما يتعلق بربط البنية التحتية. أما النموذج الرابع الذي يتناسب بشكل أوثق مع القوس الطبيعي، فكان الأكثر فائدة مع نسبة أكبر لتكامل المناطق وبأقل كلفة لربط البنية التحتية.

النموذج الأول هو "المحوري" المتمثل بمدينة كبرى واحدة. من الحسنات المحتملة لإنشاء مدينة جديدة تمركز التنمية والتحكم المركزي، مع خلق فرص عديدة لإنشاء رموز قوية وإيجابية للدولة، لكن هذا النموذج يؤدي أيضاً إلى تحديات إجرائية وسياسية واقتصادية هائلة. وعلاوةً على ذلك، يعتقد فريق البحث أن من المرجح ألا تتوفر في الضفة الغربية الأراضي المتواصلة والقابلة للبناء والملائمة والكافية لمثل هذه المدينة.

النموذج الثاني هو "ثلاثي المحاور" المتمثل بثلاث مدن كبيرة، وبالتحديد القدس والخليل ونابلس. قد يخفف مثل هذا النموذج من بعض العوائق الإجرائية والسياسية والاقتصادية للنموذج "المحوري"، إلا أن الفريق لا يزال يخشى من أن تقسيم ثلاثة ملايين من السكان الجدد على ثلاث مناطق قد يؤدي إلى مدن فائضة الاكتظاظ وغير قادرة على دعم المتطلبات، كما أن الأراضي المتوفرة للبناء لن تكون كافية لسلك هذا المسار بنجاح.

النموذج الثالث هو "شبكي" متمثل ببلدات ومدن متبعثرة. إن توزيع النمو الجديد بشكل متساوٍ نسبياً على كافة أنحاء الضفة الغربية جذاب من حيث المبدأ، لأنه ينشر أعباء النمو وفوائده على قدم المساواة، إلا أن التنمية المتبعثرة ربما تتطلب مساحات أكثر للبنية التحتية وبكلفة أعلى. وفي الواقع فالحاجة إلى عدد كبير من البنى التحتية سيجعل من الصعب تحديد الأولويات القومية ويجعلها مكلفة للغاية. وقد يشجع مثل هذا النمو الموزع أيضاً "البلقنة" السياسية، مما يضعف المؤسسات والمبادرات الإقليمية والقومية الأكبر.

النموذج الرابع هو "الخطي" المتمثل بسلسلة من المدن المتعددة. فالتوزيع الجغرافي والسكاني للضفة الغربية يوحي بوصل معظم المدن الكبرى على طول خط رئيسي واحد،

يغطي معظم السكان بفعالية نسبية. وقد توفر سلسلة المدن هذه تركيزاً وتوجيهاً للتنمية الاقتصادية الجديدة بينما تساعد على إعادة إحياء المراكز التاريخية الرئيسية القائمة. ومن خلال حث كل منطقة مدينية على النمو في شكل خطي أو "غصن" يربطها بالخط الرئيسي الوطني، يصبح الشكل الصغير والمستدام للمدن مفضلاً على النمو غير الموجه وغير المقيد. ويربط هذا النموذج النمو بالأنماط الطبيعية والسكنية القائمة، بالإضافة إلى احتمال خلق رمز وطني قوي عبر البنية التحتية المتواصلة، بدلاً من معالم هندسية فردية مكلفة ومسرفة. من سيئات هذا النموذج تفضيل المناطق المركزية للضفة الغربية على حساب المناطق الشرقية والغربية، كما أنه إذا أسيء تنفيذها فقد تخلق تنمية مدينية كثيرة على طول القوس. وعلى أساس هذا التحليل، اختار الفريق النموذج "الخطي" لأنه يحتوي على أكثر الوعود.

النمو في غزة

عند وضع الخطط لاستيعاب النمو السكاني الكبير في فلسطين، ستكون من إحدى الخطوات الجلية تخفيض إلى الحد الأدنى من عبء النمو في قطاع غزة. وبالرغم من أن قطاع غزة سيشهد نمواً طبيعياً كبيراً في عدد السكان على مدى العقود التالية، إلا أن الكثافة السكانية تبلغ الآن ٣٬٥٠٠ شخص في الكيلومتر المربع (٩٬٢٠٠ شخص في الميل المربع). وبسبب هذا الارتفاع الأولي في الكثافة السكانية، والندرة النسبية للأراضي المفتوحة، والانفصال الجغرافي بين قطاع غزة والضفة الغربية، فقد قررنا أن التخطيط المديني في قطاع غزة يتطلب أسلوباً مختلفاً جداً عن الرؤية التي وضعناها للضفة الغربية. لذا يجب أن تركز الجهود في غزة على بناء المطار والمرفأ الدوليين الجديدين، وتوصيلة المرافئ بالضفة الغربية عن طريق منشآت النقل في القوس، وتنمية بنية تحتية جديدة للسياحة على طول البحر، وإعادة التأهيل المادي والاقتصادي للمناطق المدينية في غزة. ومن جهة أخرى، يجب توجيه النمو السكاني والمديني إلى الضفة الغربية.

وصل المدن

يولي النموذج "الخطي" تركيزاً على سلسلة المدن القائمة حالياً على طول المحور المركزي من الضفة الغربية. وسيتوجه نمو السكان وتنمية المدن نحو هذا المحور. والسؤال المباشر المطروح هو كيف يتم وصل هذه المدن ببعضها.

لقد سبق وصل الأوساط التاريخية لمعظم هذه المدن عبر ما يشار إليه بالطريق ٦٠، إلا أن هذا الطريق غير ملائم لاحتياجات الدولة في المستقبل. فحركة السير سوف تبطئ حتماً عند الاقتراب من والدخول إلى كل مدينة. وبالنسبة للمسافرين مسافات أطول، قد يختفي الطريق على الجانب الجنوبي من المدينة، ثم يعود للظهور في الشمال.

إن الحاجة إلى وسيلة وصل شمالية جنوبية ووجود القوس الشمالي الجنوبي يخلقان احتمالاً مثيراً لمشروع كبير هام محاذٍ لخط القوس. وستكون الغاية الأساسية لمثل هذا

المشروع توفير وسيلة النقل الأساسية للضفة الغربية (أنظر إلى الرسم ٣) عبر خدمة مكثفة وموثوقة وسريعة لخطوط السكك الحديدية بين المدن الأساسية للضفة الغربية وصولاً إلى المطار الدولي والمدن في قطاع غزة. وسيكون مجموع طول هذه الخطوط من جنين إلى الخليل نحو ٢٠٠ كيلومتر (٧٠ ميل)، بينما يكون طول الامتداد الإضافي جنوباً إلى غزة ١٥٠ كيلومتر (٦٠ ميل).

وسيشجع بناء شبكة النقل هذه إلى بناء متوازي ومتزامن لشبكات أخرى مطلوبة للكهرباء، والغاز الطبيعي، والاتصالات السلكية واللاسلكية، والماء (أنظر إلى الرسم ٤). وقد تتداخل حديقة عامة خطية عبر الخط متأثرة بالسمات الطبيعية. وقد تعطي هذه المجموعة من المشاريع قوة كبيرة رمزية للدولة الجديدة. ونشير إلى كامل ذلك بمجرد "القوس."

بالرغم من أن خطاً للسكك الحديدية قد يشكل الجزء الرئيسي من البنية التحتية القومية، إلا أنه لا يستطيع توفير كافة أنواع النقل المطلوبة. فمن ناحية التنقل بالسيارات، ستكون هناك حاجة إلى المواصلات السريعة عبر طريق عام، ليس فقط للمقيمين الذين بإمكانهم شراء سيارة إنما أيضاً للسواح والشخصيات البارزة والمسؤولين الحكوميين إلخ. وسوف تلبي هذه الطريق العام أيضاً حاجات الاسعاف، والعناصر الأمنية والعسكرية، وكافة أنواع آليات الصيانة والتصليح. وبالإضافة إلى ذلك، وبالرغم من أن شبكة السكك الحديدية يجب أن تستعمل كوسيلة للشحن، إلا أنه من المرجح أن تحمل الشاحنات نسبة كبيرة من الشحنات،

الرسم ٣
خط السكك الحديدية بين المدن

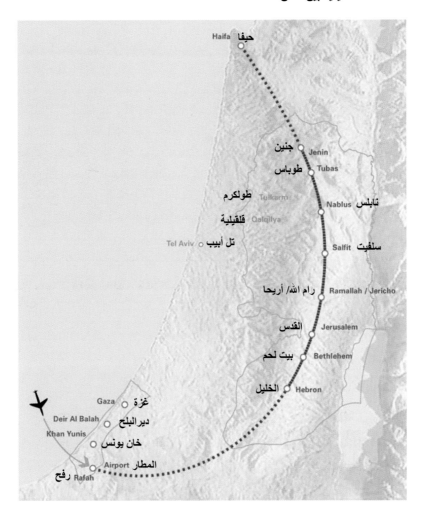

إن البنية التحتية الحاسمة على طول القوس هي خط سريع للسكك الحديدية يربط كافة المدن الأساسية في قطاع غزة والضفة الغربية، بما في ذلك محطة في المطار الدولي، ويستغرق عبوره ٩٠ دقيقة أو أكثر بقليل. ويجعل خط السكك الحديدية من النقل العام أولوية قومية بينما يوطد "الجذع" في ممر البنية التحتية القومية.

إبتداءً من شحنات صغيرة في سيارات الفان وصولاً حتى حاويات تحمَّل على عربات مقطورة. وستتطلب عمليات الشحن هذه طرقاً جيدة أيضاً. ولتلبية تلك الاحتياجات بطريقة متماشية مع الأهداف التنموية الأوسع للقوس، نقترح إنشاء طريق مزوَّدة ببوابات لجباية الرسوم، وبمجازات (مسارب) أقل عدداً، وبمخارج ومداخل محدودة جداً، ربما واحد أو إثنان لكل مركز مديني.

الرسم ٤
البنى التحتية الخمسة

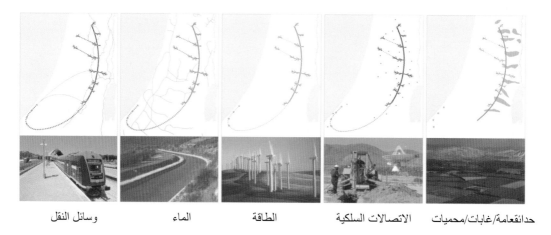

| وسائل النقل | الماء | الطاقة | الاتصالات السلكية | حدائق عامة/غابات/محميات |

القوس هو الخط الجذعي المقترح للبنية التحتية القومية الفلسطينية الذي يصل قطاع غزة والضفة الغربية. وهو يتشمل على خط سريع للسكك الحديدية، ووسيلة لنقل الماء، وتوليد ونقل الطاقة، وخطوط الاتصالات السلكية واللاسلكية، وحديقة عامة سلسلية. وتتألف كل بنية من البنى التحتية من أغصان جانبية شرقية غربية تكون هيكلا للتنمية السلسلية في كل منطقة مدينية وللمساحات المفتوحة للحدائق العامة والغابات والمحميات والمزارع.

من المفترض أن يكون إنشاء مطار دولي يربط فلسطين بالعالم ذات أهمية كبيرة لبناء هوية الدولة الجديدة واقتصادها. ولقد افترضنا أيضاً أنه لأسباب أمنية سيكون من الضروري وجود المطار الفلسطيني الرئيسي في قطاع غزة بدلاً من الضفة الغربية. وهناك أيضاً حاجة موازية إلى مرفأ دولي جنوب مدينة غزة. وستوفر مواصلات القوس بالسكك الحديدية والطرق سرعة تنقل الركاب والشحنات من المطارات والمرافئ وإليها لكافة أنحاء فلسطين. أخيراً، بالرغم من أن الهدف الأولي للبنية التحتية لقوس النقل هو تأمين المواصلات الداخلية، إلا أنه في النهاية سيوفر العمود الفقري للسفر والنقل البري بين العواصم الدولية عمان وبيروت والقاهرة ودمشق، وفي نهاية المطاف حيفا وتل أبيب وبئر السبع. ويمكن وضع نقاط الحدود الدولية في جنين وطولكرم وقلقيلية وجنوب الخليل وشرق أريحا. ويمكن تركيز الاستثمار في البنية التحتية على وصل هذا المحيط بجذع القوس.

تعزيز النمو "الخطي"

إن العرف التقليدي يوحي بوضع كل محطة جديدة على طول القوس في الوسط التاريخي لكل مدينة قائمة، إلا أن مفهوم القوس يتعمد وضع كل محطة على مسافة تبعد ما بين ٥ كيلومترات و ٤٠ كيلومتراً (٢-١٥ ميل)، من الوسط التاريخي (أنظر إلى الرسم ٥)، وذلك لعدد من الأسباب. أولاً، نظراً لعدم وجود أي بنية تحتية للسكك الحديدية في البلدات والمدن الفلسطينية، فإن التكاليف والتعطيلات المتمثلة بخرق حقوق المرور والبنية التحتية المطلوبة للسكك الحديدية بين المدن، ستكون مرتفعة بشكل غير مقبول. ثانياً، إن وجود المحطة في

وسط المركز القائم سيعزز إرتفاع نسب الكثافة والاكتظاظ في أماكن سبق أن كانت مكتظة؛ وازدياد الضغط مع الزمن على تدمير المباني والأحياء التاريخية من أجل تشييد المباني

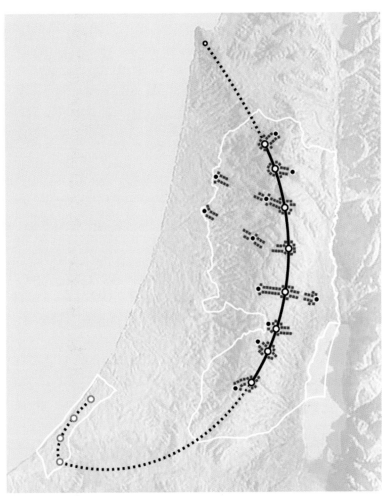

تقع كل محطة سكك حديدية استراتيجياً على طول القوس لتنشيء خطاً شرقياً غربياً من النمو المديني بين الوسط التاريخي ومنطقة المحطة الجديدة تربطهما جادة عبور (يبلغ طولها عادة من ١٥ حتى ٤٠ كيلومتراً) للنقل السريع بالباص وسيارات الأجرة (التاكسي). ويمكن تنمية أحياء جديدة على طول الجادة وبشكل متعاقب لاستيعاب ما يعادل ٣ ملايين نسمة خلال السنوات الـ١٥ التالية. إن هذا النموذج ينشئ المواقع وكذلك الحدود للنمو المديني على المدى الطويل، مما يضمن حماية المساحات الوطنية المفتوحة.

الأكثر كثافة وعلواً. ثالثاً، سيخلق إنشاء محطة في الوسط التاريخي ضغطاً نحو النمو الدائري حول الوسط، مما يزيد من صعوبة الوصول إلى الوسط. وفي المقابل فإن الموقع

البعيد المقترح للمحطة سوف يشجع نمط توسع خطي منظم من الوسط التاريخي للمدينة على طول شريان مجهز بالنقل العام ومصمم لتلبية حاجات التنمية على المدى البعيد.

من إحدى المشاكل الدائمة التي تواجهها البلدان النامية خصوصاً الميل إلى المركزية المفرطة، بحث تؤول المنطقة المدينية إلى أن مدينة ضخمة تستنزف الاستثمار والنمو الاقتصادي من كافة المناطق الأخرى. وأحد أهداف مفهوم القوس هو التخفيض إلى الحد الأدنى من الفروقات بين مختلف المدن لتشجيع الاستثمار والنمو الأكثر إعتدالاً على طول خط القوس، وبالتالي في كافة أنحاء الضفة الغربية وغزة.

إن استراتيجية وضع منطقة المحطة الجديدة على مسافة من الوسط التاريخي للمدن مبنية على أساس بناء جادة للوصل بينهما (أنظر إلى الرسم ٦). وقد تتألف هذه الجادة من طريق واحد أو سلسلة من الممرات المتوازية مختلفة الحجم والغاية. إن بنية الجادة تنظم النمو من الوسط التاريخي نحو المحطة، إذ أن من المرجح أن ينمو الوسط، بل أن يكتظ على المدى القصير مع عودة الموجة الأولى من اللاجئين. ويمكن توجيه وطأة التوسع على طرفي الجادة حيث يمكن تنمية الأحياء الجديدة.

يقدم مفهوم القوس الوعد بنظام للمساحات الوطنية المفتوحة التي يمكن تنميتها من خلال دمج نظامين بيئيين قائمين هما من جهة السمات الطبيعية الواسعة للحقول الزراعية والمدرجات الزراعية والبساتين والمزارع والق ى المرتبطة بها، ومن جهة أخرى، مجموعة الغابات المحمية والمحميات الطبيعية التي ﺒ ﺪﺪها في كافة أنحاء الضفة الغربية. إن الطابع الخاص للمساحات المفتوحة ووﺠ ﺎﻟﻬﺎ تتطلب الدراسة الدقيقة، لكن من الناحية المبدئية، يجب أن يكون من الممكن ﺍﻥ ﻳﺘﻨﺰه المرء أو أن يركب الدراجة لمسافة قصيرة على طول الحديقة السلسلية داخل منطقة مدينة مثل نابلس أو بيت لحم؛ أو بشكل أكثر طموحاً أن يتنزه أو يركب الدراجة على طول الامتداد الكامل للقوس.

الأحياء الجديدة

في صميم مفهوم القوس استقرار عدة ملايين من الأشخاص في أحياء جديدة على جانبي جادات العبور الجديدة. ويمكن هكذا معايرة عملية الإنشاء النامية والمتتابعة للأحياء الجديدة ليجاري نمو عدد السكان وعودة اللاجئين.

الرسم ٦
مشهد جوي لـ"القوس"

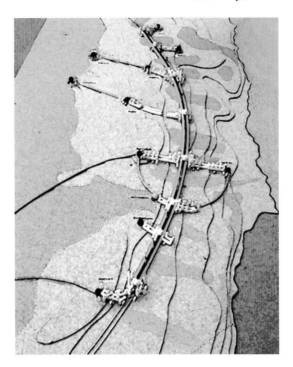

مشهد جوي يبين القوس داخل الضفة الغربية، بما في ذلك خطوط جذوع
البنية التحتية، والجادات أو "الأغصان" بين مناطق المحطات الجديدة
(النقاط البيضاء) والأوساط التاريخية (النقاط السوداء)، والمنتزهات
ومحميات المساحات الوطنية المفتوحة.

بالإضافة إلى الإسكان، ستشمل الأحياء الجديدة الحوانيت، والأسواق، والمدارس،
والعيادات، والمساجد وغيرها من الهياكل الدينية، والحدائق العامة الصغيرة، والمنشآت
الثقافية (أنظر إلى الرسم ٧). وقد يتراوح ارتفاع المباني الاعتيادية من دورين حتى ستة
أدوار. وقد تمتد هذه الأحياء إلى مسافة معينة من الجادة، وعادةً على منحدرات التلال
الظاهرة. ويجب ألا تبلغ هذه المسافة أكثر من كيلومترين (ثلاثة أرباع الميل)، أي ما يعادل
نزهة لمدة ١٥ دقيقة على القدمين، من الجادة من أجل الحث على استعمال النقل العام وعدم
الاعتماد على السيارات الخاصة. ويجب تواجد الوظائف عملياً في كافة النقاط على طول
الجادة، بالرغم من أن طبيعة الوظائف ستختلف من بين النقاط.

على طول جادات الوصل، يمكن إنشاء المساكن الجديدة، والمناطق التجارية، ومباني
المكاتب، والفنادق متوسطة الحجم، والمؤسسات الحكومية، والقنصليات، والمدارس،
والمنشآت الثقافية. وقد تكون المباني هنا أعلى منها في الأحياء الخلفية وقد تشمل المباني
متوسطة الارتفاع المجهزة بالمصاعد، أو حتى المباني الشاهقة في الحالات الملائمة. وقد
يكون الارتفاع الاعتيادي من خمسة إلى عشرة أدوار.

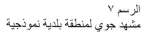

الرسم ٧
مشهد جوي لمنطقة بلدية نموذجية

مشهد جوي يبين نمط النمو البلدي النموذجي على طول جادة العبور (الأزرق)، إنطلاقًا من الوسط التاريخي (أعلى اليسار) وإمتدادًا حتى منطقة المحطة الجديدة (أدنى اليمين)، كما ويبين الطريق التاريخي رقم ٦٠ (في الأعلى)، والبنية التحتية الجديدة لسكك الحديد والماء والطاقة والطرق والمنتزهات على طول خط القوس.

بناءً على مراجعة أولية جداً، نعتقد أن هناك أرضاً كافية لبناء جادة بين كل من المحطات الجديدة والأوساط التاريخية لاستيعاب المليونين من السكان الجدد بمعدل الكثافة السكانية المقترحة لـ١٢,٠٠٠ شخص في الكيلومتر المربع (٣٠,٠٠٠ شخص في الميل المربع). ومن الممكن إسكان مليون آخر عن طريق زيادة الكثافة في المناطق المكتظة بالمباني حول المركز و/أو بطريقة طوعية في البلدات الأصغر حجماً.

يجدر التأكيد على أنه بالرغم من أن هذه الأرقام تعكس التقديرات الديموغرافية حتى سنة ٢٠٢٠، إلا أن القوس يستهدف إنشاء هيكلية لاستيعاب نمو عدد السكان الفلسطينيين والتنمية المدينية على المدى الطويل. إن تكون المناهج التالية مجتمعة بما فيها الكثافة المدينية والنقل العام والمساحات المفتوحة المحمية لقادرة على دعم ودوام بيئة يمكن العيش فيها وقابلة للنمو لأجيال قادمة.

التكاليف والفوائد الاقتصادية المباشرة من بناء القوس

شأنه شأن خيارات التنمية الموصوفة في "بناء دولة فلسطينية ناجحة"، سيتطلب بناء العناصر الأساسية للقوس استثماراً طائلاً للموارد الاقتصادية. وفي الوقت نفسه، إن التوظيف المرتبط بمثل هذه المشاريع الكبيرة لتنمية البنية التحتية هام بحد ذاته، بالإضافة إلى الفوائد الاقتصادية والاجتماعية لهذه المشاريع على المدى الطويل.

إننا نركز على تكاليف البناء في مجالين: النقل وبالتحديد خط للسكك الحديدية وطريق عام على طول الامتداد الأساسي للقوس، و"الجادات" التي تصل المراكز السكنية التاريخية بمحطات القطار الواقعة على القوس، ومحطات القطار بحد ذاتها، ومحطات العبور على طول الجادات وكذلك المساكن للمهاجرين إلى دولة فلسطينية جديدة. ولأسباب نوقشت في "القوس: بنية منهجية لدولة فلسطينية"، لا تشمل تقديرات التكاليف كلفة شراء الأراضي، سواء كان ذلك للطرق أو السكك الحديدية أو المحطات أو المساكن. وكافة التكاليف منقولة بالقيمة الاسمية (أي السنة الحالية) للدولار الأميركي.

نقدر أن تبلغ تكاليف بناء الأجزاء الرئيسية لخط السكك الحديدة في القوس، من طولكرم في الشمال إلى قطاع غزة في الجنوب، نحو ٣٫٣ بلايين دولار أميركي، بما فيها قطارات السكة الحديدية وقافلاتها. وقد تبلغ كلفة الطريق العام الرئيسي على طول القوس نحو ٢٫١ بليون دولار أميركي، بينما يكلف بناء جادات الوصل نحو ٢٧٥ مليون دولار أميركي. وتبلغ كلفة بناء المحطات الرئيسية للسكك على القوس والمحطات الصغيرة على طول جادات الوصل نحو ٣٠٠ مليون دولار أميركي. وهكذا نقدر أن يكون مجموع تكاليف البنية التحتية الأساسية للسكك الحديدية والطرق نحو ٦ بلايين دولار أميركي.

في ما يتعلق بتكاليف الإسكان، افترضنا أن معظم الفلسطينيين سيعتمدون على جهودهم ومواردهم الخاصة لبناء أو تحسين المساكن. وفي الوقت نفسه، ندرك أن تدفقاً كبيراً للمهاجرين قد تكون له آثار كبيرة على أسواق المساكن المحلية مما قد يحدو بالجهات المانحة التدخل بهدف التخفيف من هذه الآثار. لذا نشمل تقديراً لتكاليف بناء المساكن الجديدة للعائدين. وإذا افترضنا الكثافة نفسها للمقيمين في كل مسكن كما هو الحال حالياً في قطاع غزة والضفة الغربية (٦٫٤ أشخاص لكل وحدة) وتقديرنا لـ ٦٣٠,٠٠٠ مهاجر جديد على مدى عشر سنوات، فستكون هناك الحاجة إلى ١٠٠,٠٠٠ وحدة سكنية إضافية لإيواء هذا التدفق. وبمعدل كلفة نقدره بـ ٢٥,٠٠٠ دولار أميركي لكل وحدة سكنية، يبلغ المجموع ٢٫٥ بليون دولار أميركي.

إن بناء البنية التحتية للنقل والمساكن سيساهم في توظيف عمال البناء الفلسطينيين، مما يزيد من نسبة العمالة ودخل الأسرة. ولقد قدرنا العدد المحتمل لوظائف البناء التي يولدها هذا الإنفاق بقسمة مجموع قيمة الإنفاق المتوقع على البناء بالدولارات على تقدير إجمالي إنتاج البناء لكل عامل بالدولارات، استناداً إلى إحصائيات التوظيف والدخل القومي من الدول العربية المجاورة. بناءً على مجموع استثمار قدره ٨٫٥ بلايين دولار أميركي، ستكون هناك حاجة إلى ٥٣٠,٠٠٠ سنة فردية من عمالة البناء تقريباً لإتمام المشاريع الموصوفة هنا، وذلك بناءً على البيانات الأردنية. وإذا اعتمدنا البيانات المشابهة في مصر حيث إنتاجية

العمالة في البناء أدنى مما هي في الأردن، نقدر أن العمل سيتطلب ٨٠٠,٠٠٠ سنة فردية. وإذا افترضنا أن المشاريع الأساسية للقوس ستُبنى على مدى خمس سنوات فتقديرنا هو أن المستوى الضروري للاستثمار المالي سيوظف من ١٠٠,٠٠٠ إلى ١٦٠,٠٠٠ فلسطيني سنوياً خلال هذه المدة.

إننا نشدّد أن هذه التقديرات للتكاليف والوظائف تقريبية. ونحن نهدف إلى الاستعانة بها كمرجع للبحث في مدى المساعدة المالية التي ستكون مطلوبة من المجتمع الدولي للمساعدة على إنشاء دولة فلسطينية ناجحة. فالتقديرات الأكثر دقة ستتطلب دراسات رسمية للتكاليف تشمل تقييمات مفصلة للاحتياجات. وعلاوةً على ذلك، لا يشمل أي من تقريري مؤسسة راند اللذين نوقشا هنا تكاليف كافة التغييرات والتحسينات المؤسساتية الكبرى في البنية التحتية والتي ستكون مطلوبة من أجل دولة فلسطينية ناجحة.

التحديات الاجتماعية والسياسية لاستيعاب اللاجئين

كما سبق أن وصفنا، تم تصميم مفهوم القوس لمعالجة الاحتياجات المادية والاقتصادية للشعب الفلسطيني الآن وفي المستقبل، بدون إيلاء اهتمام خاص بما إذا كان سبب نمو السكان عائداً إلى التزايد الطبيعي أو عودة اللاجئين. وفي الوقت نفسه، من الواضح أن استيعاب أعداد كبيرة من المهاجرين سيمثل تحديات في وجه دولة فلسطينية جديدة بطرق تتخطى الاستيعاب المادي للمقيمين الإضافيين. ويجدر البحث جلياً في هذه التحديات.

لذا سنقوم في إطار مشروع القوس بالبحث في سلسلة هامة من التحديات الاجتماعية والسياسية والاقتصادية التي ستواجهها الدولة الفلسطينية وهي تعالج مسألة استيعاب أعداد كبيرة من المهاجرين الجدد الذين من المرجح أن يأتوا أساساً من مجموعات اللاجئين في لبنان وسوريا والأردن.

سيتمثل التحدي الأساسي في سلسلة من المعضلات:

- ستعتمد شرعية الحكومة الجديدة جزئياً على نجاحها في إعادة توطين عدد كبير من اللاجئين الفلسطينيين، إلا أن تدفق عدد كبير من اللاجئين سيضع ضغوطاً على مؤسسات الدولة بطريقة ستتحدى قدرتها على الحكم الجيد وبالتالي شرعيتها.

- علاوةً على ذلك، قد تجبر الحكومة التي تجاهد لإثبات شرعيتها على الطلب من السكان الحاليين غير اللاجئين في فلسطين القبول بأن يكونوا أقلية عندما تنضم أعداد كبيرة من اللاجئين العائدين إلى السكان اللاجئين الحاليين.

- سيكون للحكومة الجديدة مصلحة في ضمان الالتحام الاجتماعي على الصعيد القومي، مما يدعو إلى توزيع العائدين بطريقة لا تديم الانقسامات الاجتماعية، إلا أن العائدين سيريدون الاستقرار حيث سبق أن استقرت أسرهم وقد يعارضون الحكومة التي تسعى الى تفرقتهم.

- قد لا تكون الحكومة قادرة على قصر جهودها لإعادة توطين اللاجئين العائدين من الخارج لأن العدد الكبير من اللاجئين الذين ما زالوا يعيشون في المخيمات داخل فلسطين ولأجيال عديدة، بالإضافة إلى مرحلين كثيرين لا يحملون صفة اللاجئين الشرعية رغم أنهم بالفعل لاجئون، لا بد أن يطالبوا أن يعاملوا بالمساواة مع العائدين. وسيثقل هذا كاهل الحكومة الجديدة بمسؤوليات أكبر.
- أخيراً، على الحكومة الجديدة أن تتغلب على التشكك العميق الذي يراود العائدين من لبنان والأردن وسوريا في سلطة الدولة، حتى بينما تسعى إلى تخفيض اعتماد هذه الفئات على الدولة.

من الناحية العملية، إن وضع الخيارات السياسية المفصلة لمعالجة كافة هذه القضايا لم يكن ضمن إطار هذا التحليل. وعلاوةً على ذلك، فإن طبيعة هذه القضايا الاجتماعية والسياسية تدعو إلى معالجتها محلياً بطرق تتماشى مع الخيارات الوطنية وواقع بنود التسوية التي سوف تنشأ بموجبها الدولة الفلسطينية المستقلة. وفي الوقت نفسه، نعتقد أن البحث المفصل في هذه القضايا والذي نقدمه في "القوس: بنية منهجية لدولة فلسطينية" سيساعد على تحفيز النقاش حول هذه المسائل والتخطيط لها، ليمكن معالجتها بسرعة وبفعالية عندما تقتضي الظروف.

تحقيق التنمية الناجحة

من الضروري أن تنجح الدولة الفلسطينية في حال إنشائها. والهدف من تحليل مؤسسة راند هو وصف الخطوات التي يستطيع إتخاذها الفلسطينيون والإسرائيليون والأميركيون والمجتمع الدولي من أجل ضمان نجاح الدولة الفلسطينية المستقلة الجديدة.

ستبدأ الدولة الفلسطينية المستقلة من مواضع قوة كثيرة تشمل شعباً ملتزماً بنجاح دولته، وحسب استطلاعات الرأي، يريد العيش جنباً إلى جنب وبسلام مع إسرائيل، شعب يتمتع بمستوى جيد نسبياً من العافية والعلم مقارنة مع بلدان أخرى في الجوار ذات مستويات التنمية الاقتصادية مماثلة. أضف إلى ذلك أن البنية التحتية للصحة والتعليم قد ثبتت مرونتها وتكيفها حتى أما تحديات سياسية واقتصادية صارمة. وتجدر الإشارة إلى الدرجة القوية من المساواة بين الجنسين في حصيلة التعليم. وفي مجالي الصحة والتعليم وغيرهما، ستتمكن دولة فلسطينية من الاستفادة من قاعدة قوية من المؤسسات الحكومية وغير الحكومية ومن العديد من المهنيين ذوي المهارات العالية.

وفي الوقت نفسه، ستواجه الدولة الجديدة تحديات هامة. وبشكل أساسي، يجب أن تحقق الدولة الجديدة الأمن داخل حدودها، وأن توفر السلامة الاعتيادية لسكانها، وأن تخلو من أي أعمال تخريب متطرف أو استغلال أجنبي، وألا تشكل أي تهديد أمني على إسرائيل، وهي أوضاع وحالات مفقودة على الأقل منذ بداية الانتفاضة الثانية عام ٢٠٠٠. ويجب أن تؤسس الدولة حاكمية فعّالة وتحافظ على دوامها، بدلاً من الحكم الفاسد والتعسفي الذي ساد منذ عام ١٩٩٤. وسيكون في الدولة عدد كبير ومتنامٍ بسرعة من السكان على نسبة مرتفعة من الإعالة (أي نسبة الأطفال والمسنين إلى العاملين)، وهجرة مرجحة لأعداد كبيرة من الفلسطينيين من الخارج؛ وستبدأ ببنية تحتية طبيعية غير كافية لتلبية احتياجات سكانها الحاليين، ناهيك عن استيعاب عدد كبير من اللاجئين العائدين. وستواجه فلسطين تحدٍ هائلاً لتحقيق نمو اقتصادي كبير ودائم.

إننا نرى أن تنفيذ السياسات والبرامج في إطار تلك التي تمت التوصية بها في "بناء دولة فلسطينية ناجحة" و"القوس: بنية منهجية لدولة فلسطينية" ضروري ولو أنه غير كافٍ

لنجاح الدولة الفلسطينية المستقلة على مدى العقد الأول من تأسيسها. وسيتطلب مثل هذا التنفيذ بدوره التزامات سياسية ومالية قوية من المجتمع الدولي.

وكمرجع لتحديد حجم التمويل الذي قد يكون مطلوباً من الجهات المانحة الدولية لضمان نجاح التنمية الفلسطينية، بحثنا في حالتي البوسنة وكوسوفو حيث استثمر المجتمع الدولي في الآونة الأخيرة مبالغ كبيرة جداً لإعادة الإعمار بعد إنتهاء النزاع. فكما في الضفة الغربية وقطاع غزة، تعرض هذان الكيانان للضرر كبير من النزاعات. ولقد جذبت البوسنة وكوسوفو نسبة كبيرة من الاهتمام والمساعدة الدوليتين؛ ولقد أحرز كلاهما بعض النجاح في إنشاء حكومات ديموقراطية وفي إعادة إحياء الاقتصاد المحلي.

في الفصل حول التنمية الاقتصادية في "بناء دولة فلسطينية ناجحة"، قدمنا وصفاً لمخططات نمو اقتصادي لمستويات من الاستثمار الرأسمالي بنحو ٣٫٣ بلايين دولار أميركي سنوياً، أو قرابة ٣٣ بليون دولار أميركي على مدى العقد الأول من الاستقلال (بما في ذلك معظم أو كل احتياجات الاستثمار المحددة التي نصفها في تحاليلنا). وعلى المستوى الفردي، يمثل هذا معدلاً سنوياً قدره نحو ٧٦٠ دولاراً أميركياً للفرد. وعلى سبيل المقارنة، يمثل هذا نحو ٢٫٥ مرة ضعف قيمة المعونة الدولية للفرد التي تم تقديمها للضفة الغربية وقطاع غزة عام ٢٠٠٢ (٣٠٠ دولار أميركي تقريباً)، وأقل من ضعف المبلغ الفردي المقدم لكوسوفو خلال السنتين الأولتين بعد إنتهاء النزاع (٤٣٣ دولاراً أميركياً)، وأكثر بقليل فقط من المبلغ الفردي المقدم للبوسنة خلال السنتين الأولتين بعد إنتهاء النزاع (٧١٤ دولاراً أميركياً).

وهكذا هناك سوابق مماثلة حديثة من المعونات الدولية للفرد تقارب ما نقدر أنه سيكون مطلوباً في فلسطين. وفي الوقت نفسه، إن مستوى الالتزام الدولي الذي نصفه لهو أعلى (من حيث الفرد والمستوى المطلق) ومستمر لمدى أطول من الزمن مقارنة بالمساعدات المقدمة للبوسنة أو كوسوفو أو أي معونات دولية أخرى في الآونة الأخيرة. وسيتطلب تحقيق هذا الالتزام تعاوناً دولياً منظماً.

التطلع إلى المستقبل

حتى تاريخ كتابة هذه الخلاصة، لا تزال التوقعات لإنشاء دولة فلسطينية مستقلة غير أكيدة. فإنتباه الولايات المتحدة، التي يبدو بدونها التفاوض على التسوية بين الفلسطينيين والإسرائيليين غير محتمل، مركز بدرجة أولى على العراق. وبالرغم من ذلك، تبقى مجموعة حاسمة من الفلسطينيين والإسرائيليين، بالإضافة إلى الولايات المتحدة وروسيا والاتحاد الأوروبي والأمم المتحدة، ملتزمة بهدف إنشاء دولة فلسطينية. والأحداث الأخيرة بما فيها وفاة ياسر عرفات وإنتخاب محمود عباس بديلاً له، قد تحوّل هذا الاحتمال إلى حقيقة أوشك للحدوث.

إن الحافز لتحاليلنا نابع من اعتقادنا الراسخ بأن الإعداد الدقيق يسهل السلام. وعندما يحين وقت السلام، سيكون هذا الإعداد عنصراً أساسياً لنجاح الدولة الجديدة، كما تبيّن من تجربة الولايات المتحدة في الآونة الأخيرة في العراق وأفغانستان. إن الغاية من عملنا هذا

هو مساعدة الفلسطينيين والإسرائيليين والمجتمع الدولي على الإعداد للوقت الذي تكون فيه الأطراف مستعدة لإنشاء دولة فلسطينية ناجحة ولإدامتها.